Welcome to Poetryland

Welcome to Poetryland

Teaching Poetry Writing to Young Children

Shelley Savren

ROWMAN & LITTLEFIELD
Lanham • Boulder • New York • London

Published by Rowman & Littlefield
A wholly owned subsidiary of The Rowman & Littlefield Publishing Group, Inc.
4501 Forbes Boulevard, Suite 200, Lanham, Maryland 20706
www.rowman.com

Unit A, Whitacre Mews, 26-34 Stannary Street, London SE11 4AB

Copyright © 2016 by Shelley Savren

All permissions regarding poems quoted in this text can be found in the back of the book.

All rights reserved. No part of this book may be reproduced in any form or by any electronic or mechanical means, including information storage and retrieval systems, without written permission from the publisher, except by a reviewer who may quote passages in a review.

British Library Cataloguing in Publication Information Available

Library of Congress Cataloging-in-Publication Data

Names: Savren, Shelley, author.
Title: Welcome to poetryland : teaching poetry writing to young children / Shelley Savren.
Description: Lanham : Rowman & Littlefield, [2016]
Identifiers: LCCN 2016014841 (print) | LCCN 2016017159 (ebook) | ISBN 9781475825220 (cloth : alk. paper) | ISBN 9781475825237 (pbk. : alk. paper) | ISBN 9781475825244 (Electronic)
Subjects: LCSH: Language arts (Early childhood) | Poetry--Study and teaching (Early childhood)
Classification: LCC LB1139.5.L35 S28 2016 (print) | LCC LB1139.5.L35 (ebook) | DDC 372.62--dc23
LC record available at https://lccn.loc.gov/2016014841

∞™ The paper used in this publication meets the minimum requirements of American National Standard for Information Sciences—Permanence of Paper for Printed Library Materials, ANSI/NISO Z39.48-1992.

Printed in the United States of America

*In Memory of
Charles Welch*

Autobiographia Literaria

When I was a child
I played by myself in a
corner of the schoolyard
all alone.

I hated dolls and I
hated games, animals were
not friendly and birds
flew away.

If anyone was looking
for me I hid behind a
tree and cried out "I am
an orphan."

And here I am, the
center of all beauty!
writing these poems!
Imagine!

—Frank O'Hara

Contents

Foreword	xi
Preface	xiii
Acknowledgments	xv
Introduction	1
1 Imagine a Purple Elephant: Teaching Grades Pre-K Through 5	17
2 Magic Poetry Pencils and Mistake Stickers— "Special Needs" Students	55
3 The Craft of Poetry: Gifted, Seminar, and Pullout Programs	65
4 Poetry Outside the Classroom	77
5 Poetry in the Face of Art: Writing in an Art Museum	85
6 Home Is Where You Sleep at Night: Homeless, Abused, and Neglected Students	97
Appendix: Additional Exercise Ideas	113
Permissions	115
Resources	119
Index	121
About the Author	125

Foreword
Tim Dewar

The only poem I remember writing in elementary school got me in trouble. At the end of fourth grade, I wrote:

Roses are red,
Violets are blue,
Sugar is sweet,
But you're not.

I wrote this in a journal my teacher forced me to keep. It was to her. I think I meant it as a kind of throwaway good-bye. What I didn't know was that Ms. Garrido would actually read the things we wrote on that last day. Phone calls had been made, and I recall my mother's hand on my collar as we walked down the school hallway.

The playground was empty, the desks vacant, even the classroom walls were bare. Ms. Garrido put my journal in front of me, open to my poem. She started talking, but all I could focus on were her eyes. They were welling up with tears as she explained her feelings when she read my poem.

I apologized.

It was a sincere apology. I don't think I knew until that awkward conference that my words could hurt an adult, that they had any power at all. Words were just these things I threw around, but I learned words could make things happen in the world. Words could hurt, and words could heal.

There is a better way for young students to learn these lessons about the power of language, and you are holding it in your hands. Shelley Savren's *Welcome to Poetryland: Teaching Poetry Writing to Young Children* provides teachers with a delightfully playful approach to sharing the magic of poetry with students. Filled with exquisite samples from poets young and old, this book offers guidance on the details (poetry position!) and the big picture (What does success look like?) of teaching poetry writing. Her advice has been honed in countless classrooms with students of all ages, types, and abilities.

As an accomplished poet herself, Shelley Savren knows how poets and poetry work. What sets this book apart, though, is that she also knows kids. A simile isn't a strange, technical vocabulary word. It's a tree as tall as a monster. Revision isn't just a step in the writing process. It's a "delicate business" for writer, audience, and teacher. The lessons narrated in this book show how to support students as they come to see the world as poets do, using the tools poets use, to express experiences and feelings universal to us all.

Most importantly, though, Shelley Savren shares a love of the magic of poetry that is alive to the possibilities of words, kids' words, poets' words, *our* words, to make the world a better place. Had I known that in fourth grade, I think I would have quite different memories of poetry in elementary school.

Tim Dewar
Director of the South Coast Writing Project, an Affiliated Site
of the California and National Writing Projects

Preface

In 2010, I received an email from Ruth Millar Hanley, a thirty-six-year-old married mother of two, living in Seattle, Washington. She was a student of mine for three years at Kellogg Elementary School, and I came into her classroom weekly and taught poetry writing. She found me on Oxnard College's website, where I had been teaching full time for over twenty years, and in honor of National Poetry Month, contacted me saying that she still has her poetry notebooks from third, fourth, and fifth grades, still writes poetry, and read one of her poems at her college graduation.

She wrote, "I've been wanting to contact you, just to say thank you for the gift of poetry in my life—you truly unlocked a door in me that was very impactful in my life and a tool to express emotions beyond my understanding at such a young age. I love how capable kids are of expressing through poetry what they can't express in plain text. I love that you taught us about similes and metaphors and read Walt Whitman. . . . I wanted you to know that your influence so long ago is still felt and that I still think of you with such appreciation."

Her email concluded with, "My absolute FAVORITE thing about you, and I still remember as clear as day, was when kids would read their poem and if it had a really good image in it, you would take some time to pause for a while, while we all stared at you wide-eyed, and say, 'Wow. Read that again!' That was the ultimate."

Ruth's words in that email inspired me to write this book—to record my experiences of conducting poetry-writing workshops for over twenty-five thousand students for forty years. My intention in telling these stories is to show the authenticity of each experience in order to get teachers excited about putting to use what follows: poetry-writing exercises, complete with model poems.

During the poetry-writing workshops described in this book, students have taken risks to write about their lives, to become vulnerable before their peers, and to embrace poetry as essential in their lives. They are the future's poets and audience members. My hope is that teachers will use the exercises in this book to continue to bring poetry into the lives of young students—everywhere.

Acknowledgments

I am fortunate to have had opportunities to teach poetry to over twenty-five thousand students over the past forty years, beginning in 1975, when California Poets in the Schools (CPITS) contacted me to conduct a poetry-writing workshop. I have worked with them ever since. The poets in that program have given me tremendous support and guidance over the years, and I have trained dozens of CPITS poets to work in schools and the community.

I am especially grateful to Charles Welch, formerly the Special Projects Coordinator for Chula Vista City Schools in San Diego County, California. Charles was one of those rare educators who really understood how poetry was transformative, how it was the most important part of a teaching curriculum. He kept building my program at Kellogg Elementary School (and then at Rosebank Elementary), and eventually created a "Poet in Residence" position—full-time, with benefits!

I also received grants three years in a row from the Combined Arts and Education Council of San Diego County (COMBO) through its National Endowment for the Arts (NEA) re-granting program. Matching funds were provided by the San Diego Office of Education Court and Community Schools Program. This allowed me to conduct workshops at two court schools: Harbor Summit School for homeless children and Hillcrest School for abused and neglected wards of the court.

My biggest funding source was the California Arts Council (CAC), to whom I am eternally grateful for awarding me *nine* Artist-in-Residence grants. The last six years of CAC grants (1987–1992) had matching funds provided by the San Diego Unified School District's Fine Arts Coordinator, Kay Wagner. I conducted poetry-writing workshops at several elementary schools, but primarily at Sunset View.

The workshops I did at the San Diego Museum of Art, through its Young at Art program, took place during this residency and were funded by the Maxwell H. Gluck Foundation, with additional funds from Sunset View's PTA used for transporting its students to the museum.

I conducted poetry-writing workshops in hundreds of schools throughout San Diego County until I moved to Ventura, California in 1992, when I began teaching full-time at Oxnard Community College. At that time, I also began conducting poetry-writing workshops in the community and in schools at all grade levels throughout Ventura County—which I have always been committed to doing, even though it was on a much smaller scale than before.

For the past twenty years, the City of Ventura Office of Cultural Affairs has granted funds to CPITS to conduct poetry-writing workshops in schools at all grade levels. I've taught in dozens of classrooms through those grants. Also, the City of Ventura awarded me five fellowships—just to write poetry—for which I am humbly grateful.

Over the years, I have also received funding to conduct poetry-writing workshops at after-school, summer school, home school, and library programs. These included Grossmont College for Kids (San Diego County, California), South Coast Writing Project's "Young Writers Camp" (Ventura County, California), after-school community center programs funded by the City of Ventura, and more. Also, Red Hen Press, the publisher of my first poetry book, hired me to conduct poetry-writing workshops in Los Angeles with grant money it received for its Writing in the Schools program.

I have taught in thousands of classrooms in San Diego, Orange, Imperial, Los Angeles and Ventura counties with funding from a wide variety of sources. Many schools used Gifted and Talented Education (GATE) funds, Title I money for disadvantaged students, and Special Education funds. I am also grateful to several newspapers and magazines, including the *San Diego Union-Tribune*, *Los Angeles Times*, *San Diego Magazine*, and *Ventura County Star* for feature articles that promoted my programs.

The system trusted me. The administrators trusted me. The teachers trusted me. One principal, Ed Jones from Hueneme School District in Ventura County, California, hired me expressly to teach fourth-graders so that their writing scores would improve on their national tests. And they *did*. He understood that if you get kids excited about writing, they will want to write, and their writing will improve.

Another principal, Jon Cohee at Fred Williams School, also in Hueneme School District, continued to support my program on a large scale for many years. He knew how essential it was for students to express themselves through poetry.

Many teachers have contacted me year after year to teach poetry writing in their classrooms, convinced that this was the best language arts lesson for their students' writing. Liz Hoppe, who won Teacher of the Year for Ventura County in 2014, was one of them, and I taught her students at elementary and middle schools in Hueneme School District. In addition, I've conducted dozens of in-service workshops for elementary-school teachers on teaching poetry writing to their students and facilitated workshops at the CPITS annual symposiums.

I have never had a hard time convincing educators or administrators that teaching poetry writing works. Deep down, everyone wants to express him or herself. Poetry writing also works for my students because my excitement for poetry is contagious. Teachers have easily caught this excitement, too, and I am thankful for their partnership in bringing poetry into the lives of their students.

My students have given me so much to write about. They have trusted me and have written with me. I am always seeking more experiences where I can learn what students have to teach me. In the end, it is the students to whom I owe a debt of gratitude. I thank them. I thank everyone who has supported my poetry-writing workshops along the way.

MY GRATITUDE

Once upon a time, there was a little girl who dreamed about teaching poetry to everyone she met. She grew up, and her dream came true. Thank you to:

- Oxnard College and Ventura County Community College District for granting me a sabbatical to write this book
- the California Arts Council for so many years of financial support
- all the teachers who welcomed me into their classrooms
- all the California Poets in the Schools poets who share my work and vision
- poet Bruce Weigl for his support throughout the process of moving this book toward publication
- fellow poets Richard Newsham, Michelle Bitting, Vernard Maxam, and Elijah Imlay for encouragement and critical feedback on this book
- David Magallanes, Richard Newsham, and Elijah Imlay for many hours of copy editing and proofreading
- Charles Welch and Kay Wagner for their endless funding
- COMBO of San Diego, Ventura Arts Council, the City of Ventura Office of Cultural Affairs, and all the other numerous funding sources that kept my workshops going over the years

- Principals Jon Cohee, Ed Jones, and so many others who funded my programs
- thousands of students, young and old, for trusting my guidance and taking a journey with me through "Poetryland"

May poetry fill your hearts forever and ever!

Introduction

Teaching Students to Write Poetry

Anyone who uses language can write poetry. It's important to begin all workshops with this premise and to dismiss the notion that poetry exists somewhere outside of one's self.

The whole idea behind writing poetry is not to shut out those noises that are disturbing and distracting, but rather to become immersed in the surrounding elements; to open up all five senses and take in all that is there—to swim in it, swallow it, digest it thoroughly, and then to go beyond that sensory data to the warehouse of experiences that students can draw upon. If students sit with a memory or an experience, they can discover the emotion inside it and create images from there. This is the moment when a poem is conceived; this is the place where the muse dwells.

Magic Must Occur

Teaching young people to write poetry entails a great deal more than merely teaching technique. Some kind of magic also has to occur. Students need to be given the freedom to explore, to break down boundaries, to create worlds. They need permission to break the rules—not just of grammar—but of linear thinking and to make connections outside of the logical realm, which is what metaphor usually does.

Poetry, like all art, is self-expressive. It's easy. Everyone has thoughts, feelings, and ideas. Students just need permission to speak from their hearts and minds and to write. Poems are born out of an opening up, and students need to be encouraged to write about their lives, to be daring. The visiting poet or teacher provides contexts; the students create content. The visiting poet or teacher shows them colors; the students paint pictures with words.

If they learn that there is poetry in everything, they only need to find it and speak it in whatever way they choose. It doesn't matter who the students are, where they come from, or how old they are. The goal is to turn everyone on to poetry because poetry enhances the human spirit. It heals the heart, and it also heals the world.

THE CLASSROOM TEACHER'S ROLE

When a visiting poet is conducting the workshop, before she or he comes to a classroom, many teachers have already gotten their students excited about poetry. This helps tremendously. Teachers often have circulated poetry books from the school library and have begun teaching some basics. In this way, the visiting poet and teacher form a partnership, spreading the excitement of poetry.

It's important for teachers to make poetry notebooks for the students or to have composition books ready for them to write in, which the visiting poet collects at the end of the workshop, reads, and returns. Younger students are used to writing on large pieces of paper with half the page blank. The blank part (for drawing the picture) should be at the bottom, so the poem will be the most important part.

Teachers also need to handle the discipline and assist students who need help. With upper-grade levels, teachers are encouraged to write with the students and become a part of the community of writers. When teachers become engaged in the same writing activity as the students, it contributes to the magic. All of these things also apply when there is no visiting poet coming to the classroom, and the teacher is conducting the workshop.

Be Spontaneous

Most teaching of poetry writing is spontaneous. The visiting poet or teacher can incorporate whatever he or she sees in the classroom into the lesson. For example, one classroom had a shower curtain as a cupboard cover. The curtain had colorful fish on it, and the students launched into a discussion about putting water in their poems.

When students read their poems, if they happen to use a poetic concept that hasn't yet been introduced, the visiting poet or teacher can get excited and teach that technique on the spot. For example, if someone uses alliteration, just write that word on the board and guess what? Not only is that student glowing, but the next week many student poems have alliteration in them.

HOW TO READ THROUGH THESE CHAPTERS

This book is arranged by grade level and focus population. Each chapter begins with a quote from a student and an original poem by the author of this book. This is followed by a true story about working in that particular environment with that specific population. Then exercises with model poems are presented, ready for teachers to put to use, along with student poems inspired by the exercises that can also be read as model poems. Most of the lessons can be adapted for students at any age or grade level.

THE FIRST DAY OF THE WORKSHOP

The first time the visiting poet enters a classroom, she or he smiles and offers a great big "hi." This relaxes the students. The visiting poet is always animated, so the room fills with excitement. Students can call the visiting poet by his or her first name, perhaps with a title (Ms. or Mr.), to create a more intimate environment.

Whether it's the visiting poet or the teacher conducting the workshop, always begin by talking about what poetry is and write the word "poetry" on the board or document camera. The class establishes that poems are made out of words. Younger students learn that "carpenters have their hammers, and poets have their words." But they don't even need to *write* the poem. They can just say it out loud, and it's a poem.

Some students may say that poems are made out of "rhyming" words, and sometimes that's true. Up until the past century, almost all poems rhymed. But today, most poems are written in free verse. Write "free verse" on the board and explain that these kinds of poems don't have to rhyme or have a set pattern. Tell them that the poems they will be writing will be in free verse and won't rhyme.

When having this discussion with students in fourth grade and higher, search for a more extensive definition of poetry which lists the elements that comprise a poem, including the use of imagination, the five senses, detail, color, imagery, emotion, rhythm, form, and figurative language (metaphor/simile, symbolism, and personification).

Begin with the "Poetry Position"

After exploring the meaning of poetry, very young students learn the poetry position. This is a focusing technique borrowed from another poet in California Poets in the Schools, Ben Hiatt, from Sacramento. It is especially helpful when teaching four-year-old preschoolers, kindergarteners, and first- and second-graders, who often have trouble sitting still.

Basically, students shake out their hands and put their thumbs together, then their forefingers, and so on, until all of their fingers are touching and their hands form a pyramid. The students then place their hands in their laps or on their desks in the poetry position. They learn that they need to be in this position whenever the class is talking about or reading poetry. It always works.

How Poems Are Like and *Not* Like Stories

No matter what grade level you are teaching, talk about how poems are like stories and other forms of prose because they tell about something. But poems look different because all the lines don't go to the end of the page. The line lengths vary. Hold up a prose or "story" page and walk around the room with it. Then do the same with a page of poetry.

Explain that stories are often longer than poems because stories take their time, like a bedtime story. But a poem moves faster, and the reader really needs to pay attention or else she or he will miss it. Also, stories are written in paragraphs. Show students how each new paragraph is indented. But poems are written in stanzas. Write the word "stanzas" on the board. When the poets get a new idea, they don't indent; they skip a space.

Then discuss how poetry uses fewer words to say more, which is also what makes it different from prose. Therefore, each word has to be carefully chosen to convey the meaning and the language tightened, which might mean breaking the rules of grammar and not always having complete sentences. When teaching upper elementary-school grades, suggest to students that they end each line with a strong noun or verb. Also, establish that poetry has a kinship to music that is based on its cadence, which is often determined by reading the poem aloud.

WHAT POEMS EXPRESS AND WHERE IDEAS COME FROM

Ask: "What does a poem express?" The answer is "feelings"—of course. Tell the students that they also use their five senses when they write poems. Then ask, "How is a poem like music?" The answer is that they both have a beat or rhythm. Just touch on these concepts during the first lesson and then elaborate on them with each new lesson. Ask if there's anything that they can't write about in a poem. The answer is no.

Then ask: "But where do all of these ideas come from?" Students might suggest books they read, places they go to, watching TV, playing with friends at school, spending time with family, and so on. Some say from their feelings, and that's true. But the word you're looking for is "imagination." Write "imagination" on the board. This will lead to the first lesson. Tell younger students to pull their imaginations out of their pockets and put them on for poetry. Then proceed from there.

THE PROCESS

There is really no mystery to the process of writing poetry. Reading and writing poetry can be fun if students can relate to the poems and are encouraged to write from their own experiences. Deep down, everyone wants to express him or herself. And often poetry is the best way to do that. Poetry writing works when a visiting poet or teacher is excited about it. That excitement is contagious.

The process is pretty simple. First, introduce a poetic element and give an open-ended writing assignment that draws on the students' own life experiences or observations. This takes about fifteen minutes. Always read model poems by both professional, published poets and by students around their own age to bridge that gap and show them that anyone can write a poem.

Also try to choose some poems by poets from their own culture. "Culture" doesn't only mean race, religion, or national origin. The word is much bigger. For example, some students learn different languages and behaviors on the street than they learn at home. That language and those behaviors are a part of a culture. The visiting poet or teacher is an outsider to that culture but has been given permission to enter in and sit on the edge—directing, observing, and hoping for success.

For Very Young Students

For classes pre-K to second grade, the students should always come to the rug for "poetry circle." When it's time to write, one way to send them back to their desks is by the colors they're wearing. For example, if they are wearing anything orange, they can stand, jump up, and reach to catch an orange star. Or if they're wearing purple, they catch a purple star.

Using birthday months works too, and so on. After they catch their imaginary stars and put them into their imaginary pockets, they place their arms at their sides and make the tiniest circle in the whole wide world. Then they return to their seats and begin writing. This activity is important to do, since, as everyone knows, young students cannot sit long and stay attentive. And it's a great transition to the activity of writing.

Question Time and Quiet Time

Once students have been given the open-ended assignment, at all grade levels, ask if there are any questions. Once questions are answered, ask who understands the assignment. Several students might raise their hands. Choose one student to repeat the assignment and then clarify anything necessary.

It's a good idea to instruct students not to talk while they write. Some people need it to be quiet, so others need to respect that. If it's a noisy class, one technique to use is to tell them that they have two minutes to talk about their poems. Then turn out the lights and say, "On your mark, get set, WRITE!" Then turn the lights back on. It works every time. The students quiet down and begin to write.

Time to Write

Have the students write in their poetry journals for about fifteen minutes. Sometimes there are students who don't want to write or don't know what to write about. They usually just need encouragement. Stoop by their sides and talk with them about ideas for poems. Ask them questions. Sometimes you can just suggest a title or a first line, and they're off. Or if they don't like the assignment, which rarely happens, they can write about anything they want.

While they are writing, walk around, putting stickers on poems when they've written at least three lines (four for fourth-graders and five for fifth-graders). Remind them that their lines can be short to look like a poem. If younger students think they are finished with their poem, suggest that they write more, if they can. Then they can draw a picture to go with the poem.

With older students, circulate and assist students when necessary or make an encouraging comment about something they wrote. However, if a student is actively writing, it's better to not say anything that will disturb the flow of her or his thoughts.

Forget Grammar and Spelling for Now

Remind students that these are drafts, so they don't need to worry about spelling or grammar. In fact, it's important to encourage them to use inventive spelling and not look up words in their word lists, which might interrupt the flow of thought for the poem. They can always look up the correct spelling or revise their poem when they're done with their draft.

But if, for example, a second-grader absolutely cannot write without spelling a word correctly, it's better to simply spell it and not make a big deal about it, so he or she can move on. Also, encourage students to write in their native language, if it is not English, or to write in English and use words from their native language in their poems. That might make the poem more interesting and might also make it easier for some students to keep their writing flowing.

Time to Read/Share Their Poems

The last fifteen or twenty minutes of the workshop is spent reading and responding to the poems. It's essential to create a safe environment for building trust. Trust means that no one laughs at a poem unless it's meant to be funny, and while they can write whatever they want without censoring themselves, no one reads a poem that will hurt or embarrass another classmate. These are called safety rules.

Also, students should not say that they don't like something in the poem or that there is something wrong with it (especially since there's no right or wrong when writing poetry), and they should not start yelling out that they can't hear the poem. If a student is reading too softly, ask her or him to use a playground voice or say that little mice are hiding in corners in the back of the room who want to hear the poem.

If the students are in fourth grade or higher, suggest that they pretend they are on a stage and need to project their voices for the audience to hear them. Tell all students that some people have soft voices, and if they can't hear a poem, they can just sit quietly and respectfully and don't have to respond.

Offering Support

Sometimes you can offer to read the poem with a student if she or he is too shy to come up to the front of the classroom and read. Or the student can just read the poem with you from her or his seat. Begin by reading the first line. The student reads the next line and then usually forgets that someone is reading with him or her and just continues on.

Sometimes a student will cry when reading a poem, and the best thing to do is just offer support. Other students sit up and really listen, and you can tell them to be that person's friend on the playground. Sometimes, you will have to finish reading the poem, or if the student doesn't want anyone to read the rest of the poem, that's okay, too. The key thing is to make every student feel important and that her or his poem is worthy of validation. Everyone claps after someone reads a poem.

The Yardstick of Success

Although almost everyone will write a poem, no one should be forced to write or to read, for that matter. Not everyone will want to share a poem every time, and that's always fine. The important thing is to continue to encourage students to write, to suggest ideas if necessary, and to remind them that they have imaginations full of ideas for poems.

If students are participating, then the workshop is successful. But "success" is an ambiguous word. Who carries the yardstick to measure it? Success can be a preschooler dictating a line or even an image. It can be a fifth-grader reading her or his poem for the first time. Or it can be students responding thoughtfully to what other students read.

CURRICULUM AND LESSON PLANS

Even though it's important to teach spontaneously, there should always be a lesson plan; in fact, these chapters present a curriculum at all levels that covers various aspects of poetics and uses the four modalities: listening, speaking, reading, and writing for different grade levels and situations. Poetry writing should be integrated across the curriculum, throughout the year, not just as a poetry unit in June.

One selling point for doing poetry-writing workshops is that they cover many aspects of language arts, and when students write poetry, their writing skills improve in other areas as well. Also, any subject can be taught through poetry. There are poems that describe social problems, historical events, and environmental catastrophes.

If you're teaching the American Civil War, you can bring in Walt Whitman. When you teach the scientific process, you can show how people come up with a hypothesis by using their imaginations like they do when they write poems. The list goes on. Also, revising poems engages mathematical and critical thinking skills.

Here is an overview of the basic poetry-writing curriculum covered in this book:

Imagination—Poetry's First Element

The number of lessons determines how much of the poetry curriculum can be covered. But it's best to talk about the imagination as the first element of poetry. Everyone uses his or her imagination to create poems; ideas come to the imagination from everything a person does, and creativity begins there.

Everyone imagines before she or he makes choices, like imagining what an ice cream flavor will taste like before it's ordered and arrives in a cone or what clothes to wear on a hot or rainy day, and anyone can go back into her or his memories and imagine the details of what happened in the past.

A poem can recreate a real experience, can expand on that experience, or can make it into something new. Visionaries, scientists, and artists draw from both inspiration and imagination. The imagination is a tool for discovering worlds. It holds a warehouse of ideas that are just waiting to be discovered. It not only helps people invent and create, but it also helps them survive; it gives them hope and belief in possibilities.

Perception—The Five Senses

The next poetic concept in the curriculum presented in these chapters is often the use of the five senses. Putting the five senses into poems makes them come alive and seem real, so other people can relate to them. The five senses are important in life, and it's the student's job to pay attention to what she or he experiences with the five senses every day. Encourage students not to just list a sense, like "I taste whipped cream," but to make it more interesting, like saying, "Sweet cream softens my mouth." Then they are using not only the sense of taste, but also the sense of touch.

Details

Another important poetic concept is the use of details in poems. Ask students to look around the room and notice a detail that they never noticed before, something that has been there for the whole year, like a crack in the ceiling or a stain on the rug. They can notice details found on the bulletin boards or walls that display posters and student writing and artwork.

Explain that poems need rich descriptions, so the reader can imagine the scene and the feeling. When writing a poem, the less vague or abstract and the more concise and specific the poem is, the more interesting it will be. Details help the reader come inside the poem, sit down, and find her or his way around; they help people relate to the poem. Tell students, "Don't write about nature; write about a tree. Better yet, write about an oak tree, an olive tree, or a palm tree in the backyard or on the street."

Color

Then there's the concept of color used in poems. Ask, "What would a black and white world be like? What if we could only watch black and white TV, like people had to do in the past?" Everyone agrees it would be boring. Tell students that no one wants her or his poems to be in just black and white either, unless someone is writing about shadows or darkness. They can use interesting colors, too, like crimson or aquamarine or chartreuse. Instead of saying, "She wore a flower in her hair," they can say, "She wore a chartreuse carnation in her hair." It makes the flower more visual.

Feelings

One of the most vital poetic concepts is the expression of feelings. It is the heart of a poem; it's what makes poems important to write and inspiring to read. The best way to put feelings into a poem is to recreate an experience and not just state a feeling. The goal is to get readers to enter the poem and exit feeling moved in some way, to react. But the poem shouldn't tell the reader *how* to feel.

Tell students: "Don't say you're *sad*; instead, describe what happened that *made* you sad," like when the author of this book writes in her poem, "At the Window": "When I drove off/ to San Francisco at twenty-one, I left her/ sobbing at that same green window." It's stronger and more interesting than saying, "I made her sad."

To effectively express a feeling in a poem, a poet has to go beneath the surface of the words and embed feelings in between the lines; he or she has to make a situation personal. The more specifically the poet describes what happened to make him or her feel a certain way, the stronger the poem will be. The poet will feel the emotion, and the reader will be able to experience what the poet or speaker is feeling and might relate the emotion to his or her own experiences. That's what makes poetry universal.

Imagery

Imagery is also essential in poetry because it distinguishes it from other types of writing. Ask, "What is an image? What do you get when you press a button on a camera or turn on a TV?" The answer is "a picture." Ask, "If an image is something a person can see, then what would an image be in poetry?" It's a picture made out of words because a poet's tool is words.

When you write the word "image" on the board, students always notice that it comes right out of the word "imagination." Tell them that they use their imaginations to create images. Imagery is the language of poetry; it's an unusual language, a higher order of language that poets use to say something ordinary, yet different from everyday speech. Images create pictures in the readers' minds, and the language is often exquisite.

Walk up to someone in the class and tell her or him to imagine walking outside when it starts to get dark. Say, "It's getting dark. Let's go inside." Then walk up to another student and tell him or her to imagine walking outside when it starts to get dark. Say, "Night is a dark visitor." But no one talks like that. A person doesn't say, "Hey, man, night's a dark visitor." Everyone will laugh at this.

Then ask, "Which is ordinary language and which is the language of poetry?" Everyone will agree that "Night is a dark visitor" is much more interesting language and preferable for poetry. It gives the reader a picture, whatever that might be for each person. That's what images do.

Similes and Metaphors

One way to automatically create images is to use figurative language, like similes, another poetic concept presented in this book. Tell students that similes are used in poetry to compare one thing to another thing that no one would ordinarily compare it to, and the comparison might not even make sense. And when poets are comparing, they use the word "like" or "as."

First they think of an object, then a word to describe it, and then a word to compare it to. For example, they can think of the word "rain." Then they can describe it as galloping, and finally, they can compare it to a fierce horse. What they get is: "The rain is *like* a fierce horse galloping across the sky." Another example a young child might say is, "I am growing *as* fast *as* a carrot." Emphasize the words "as" and "like."

Also, introduce metaphors and explain that they do the same comparing but without using the words "like" or "as." The thing they are comparing *becomes* the thing they're comparing it to. So they would say, "The rain *is* a fierce horse galloping across the sky," or "I *am* a fast growing carrot." Another example is when poet Gary Soto writes in his poem, "Sun," "The sun is a bonnet of light."

Persona and Personification

Another poetic concept is the use of a persona. When someone writes in a persona, she or he uses the word "I" but pretends to be someone else, presenting that person's point of view. The poet feels what that person feels, experiences what that person experiences, and sees the world from his or her perspective. The poet basically walks in that person's shoes. This is one reason why readers can never assume that the speaker in the poem is the author. Another reason is that when poets write about their own experiences, they frequently embellish them in their poems.

Poets also use personification, giving human characteristics to something that isn't human. For example, in her poem "The Horses," Maxine Kumin writes, "The horses have put on/ their long fur stockings." Everyone knows that horses can't put on stockings; only people can do that.

Rhythm and Alliteration

Two of the last poetic concepts in the curriculum are rhythm and alliteration. Tell students that poems are like music. Ask, "What does music have to have?" You can give them a hint by snapping your fingers, and they'll say "beat" or "rhythm." Write the word "rhythm" on the board. Poems always have rhythm. Ask if they can dance to a poem. The answer, of course, is yes.

Talk about different ways to put rhythm into poems. One way is to use very short, staccato lines or very long lines. Sometimes this is done by creating lists. Another way is to create syllabic patterns or repeat words or lines, as Mary Oliver writes in "Wild Geese": "You do not have to be good./ You do not have to walk on your knees."

Explain that traditional poetry, written before the twentieth century, had predictable patterns called "meter." A certain pattern was established and continued to repeat, like in William Blake's poem "The Tyger," where he writes: "Tyger Tyger, burning bright,/ In the forests of the night." When read out loud, everyone can hear the accented beats in every other word.

But in free verse, patterns are not predictable. Look around the room and notice patterns, for example, borders on bulletin boards, even the American flag and plaid designs on people's clothing. Notice what's predictable and what's not. Talk about patterns in nature, like the stripes on a zebra. No two zebras have the same stripes, and no one can predict the pattern, but like patterns in free verse, everyone knows that more stripes will appear. Point out that there are patterns everywhere a person goes and that everyone has certain rhythms in his or her life, like brushing teeth every morning.

As for alliteration, just encourage students to repeat consonant sounds, for example, in his poem "The Forgotten Dialect of the Heart," Jack Gilbert writes: "Ethiopian goats standing silent in the morning light." The consonant "s" is repeated in the words "goats," "standing," and "silent." Many students use alliteration naturally, and it's a good idea to point out when they do and show how it adds music to the poem.

Form

Finally, there is form. Point out how poems look different on the page from prose or stories. Teach students from about second grade up how to scan a poem for natural breath lines by reading the poem out loud and drawing slashes whenever they take a breath. Then they can recopy the poem, starting a new line at every slash, and then omitting the slashes. Tell them that this is part of editing their poems, just like correcting spelling, omitting useless words, and adding more details.

FEEDBACK

One important thing to know is that if students are made to feel good about their writing, they'll want to keep writing. So feedback is important and is also tricky. It doesn't matter how old the students are. Always focus on what's working. Everyone's ego can be fragile. Many students have trouble separating their poems from themselves, and whether they act tough or not, they can get hurt by what they interpret as criticism.

Yet critiquing is a vital part of the process. It's also a form of validation. It's not enough to just put a sticker on the poem; students need to hear that someone in the class, besides the teacher or visiting poet, liked something about their poem and could relate to it.

Younger Students Giving Feedback

Even kindergarteners and first-graders can give feedback to their classmates. After writing, the students come to the carpet. You sit in the front and choose one student to stand on each side of you. One is in the "reading position," and the other is in the "listening position," while the rest of the class is in the "poetry position." After the reader reads, ask the listener a question about the poem, and he or she responds.

It actually helps students to listen if they know they will be asked to say what they liked or repeat what they heard. The listener then becomes the reader. Rotate like this until everyone who wants to read has read. When the last reader is ready to read, the first reader takes on the role of listener.

Older Students Giving Feedback

When older students are responding to initial drafts, simply ask one person to positively point out a detail or line that he or she liked—the more specific, the better, and then add a positive comment yourself. This form of validation encourages students to continue doing whatever others liked. For example, if you say you like the rhythm in the last two lines of the poem, that student will continue to write poems with good rhythm. The same goes with images, details, and so on.

If the workshop is longer than eight weeks, you can do more extensive revision with the students. Tell them that it's best to react as an audience, stating what they observed, what they think is working great in the poem, what confuses them, and what they would like to see changed.

REVISION

Always encourage students to revise their poems when they think they're done with their drafts. Of course, not all students choose to do this, and it's important to make sure that they know that there's nothing wrong with their poems as they are.

Actually, there is a set of guidelines in some of the following chapters that you can use when doing revision as a whole class. While the main goal is to introduce students to different aspects of poetry and get them writing, revision is an important part of the process. This is the craft part.

Embracing Craft

Craft is both hard work and ecstasy. If a student loves to write poetry, she or he will want to learn more and discover the mechanics of writing. This happens at all levels, except perhaps kindergarten and first grade, where fixing the spelling and choosing a title become the focus of revision. It's the yearning that makes the student want to speak, to eventually embrace the art form and find success in writing poetry.

Every poet deals with craft differently. Explain to students that there's no right way to revise a poem. Stress that they need to read the poem aloud to hear it, in order to know if the music is working and if the poem is saying what they want it to say. Suggest that they use natural breath lines or intuit line breaks. Caution them against using abstractions and encourage them to use specific, concrete details. In the end, the student writing the poem is in charge of deciding what to change or not change.

Of course, to become a good poet, it's important to read good poetry, not just trendy rhyming poetry written expressly for kids, which doesn't serve as good models for literature. Students need to understand that successful poetry can be simple, but must have depth and meaning.

FOLLOW-UP PROJECTS

There are several follow-up projects that you can do after the students complete their poems. You can do art activities and have poetry assemblies.

Upper-grade students can even go on field trips to libraries, art museums, or coffeehouses and read their poems.

Teachers can also compile classroom anthologies. Every student usually gets to choose her or his favorite poem, revise it or at least correct the spelling, then copy it over in his or her best handwriting or type it on a computer, print, and/or save it. Students can do this at home or in the classroom. That way, they participate in another process—a publishing process, where they have control of their work and can more easily make revisions.

Instruct students who type their poems to use a font that's easy to read and not to center the poem, but to type it flush left. Each student contributes a poem to the anthology, and the class decides on a title. Select one student to design the cover, which can be made of construction paper or thicker bond.

The anthologies are then printed and can be either stapled or spiral-bound. Every student gets a copy, and one goes to the school library. With upper elementary-school grades, the teacher can do an online anthology, or the class can work on it together or in small groups.

Teachers can also have students make poetry posters, where each student pastes her or his poem onto construction paper and designs a border around it. This makes a nice display for the classroom, the hallway, the auditorium, or the office. All of these projects are just more ways that make students proud of their poems.

THE ULTIMATE GOAL

When teaching poetry writing, always wear the "poetry hat." Dance on the table. Teach them the magic. Always fill the room with passion and get students excited about poetry. Transform the classroom into another world where anything can happen. Students can go on guided fantasies. Purple elephants can wait at the door. They can all have a truly liberating experience. Even the toughest person can find openings for expression.

The goal is to teach students how to reach into their pockets, open up their imaginations, and create something meaningful out of nothing—something that they could not say in any other way; something that perhaps they didn't even know they felt; something that found its way into a poem, a keepsake stored in their psyche that they won't ever forget.

Chapter One

Imagine a Purple Elephant
Teaching Grades Pre-K Through 5

We are Poetry Girls. Wahoo!

—Silan, first grade

"Welcome to Poetryland," by Shelley Savren

Kids scurry to the rug
and I teach the poetry position:
thumb to thumb, forefinger to forefinger.
All hands become pyramids in laps.
I read red and blue rain poems,
clouds turning into sailboats,
as kids pull similes from smiles
and shove purple elephants into pockets.

When I was in kindergarten
we sang songs in circles
but never wrote a thing except our names.
I snuck books from shelves,
read nursery rhymes to other kids,
and was caught and sentenced
to the corner far from books.

Words got me in trouble.
At home I talked too fast, too much,
was put to bed too early
with stories living in my head,
squeaking their faces
through plaid wallpaper patterns,
opening their mouths so wide
words fell face down onto my bed.

Bedtime and my three-year-old
imagines a new poem:
The sun puts on pajamas
and brushes all his teeth.
When she reaches for a book,
words tumble from the page
and we scoop them into our poetry palace,
tuck them in for pleasant dreams
and listen to their breathing, like magic.

"I want to be a poetry writer when I grow up," a second-grader, Ciara, once said. The same words were spoken years later by a fourth-grade boy. For those students, poetry was serious business, enough to make a career out of it. And why not? What a wonderful world it would be if everyone wrote poetry!

Over the past forty years, elementary-school students have always been eager to have a visiting poet come to their class because writing poetry made them feel good about themselves. A kindergarten class at Sunset View Elementary School in San Diego once designed a T-shirt with "The Poetry Lady" written on it. This was a huge role to uphold; but over the years, it became an honor that was easy to wear.

On the last day of a poetry-writing workshop at Kellogg Creative Arts Magnet Elementary School in Chula Vista, California, a second-grade classroom had a banner that stretched across the room with the words: "Welcome to Poetryland." About thirty hand-drawn trees were scattered across the banner and a "thank you" poem to the visiting poet, written by the classroom students, was hiding beneath each one.

That banner was symbolic, because over the years, "Poetryland" became the landscape where hearts and stars and flying unicorns lived, where third-grader Benito wrote, "the sun [is] milking the rainbow"; where first-grader Shawn wrote, "I ate the moon for breakfast"; and where third-grader Eric wrote, "The sun blossomed across the sky." It was also the home of snakes and poetry lions. These young students knew that all adventures must include danger and struggle in order for them to grow and achieve goals.

During workshops, secrets came out. Some students wrote about their parents' divorce or drugs in their neighborhood. Writing poetry was a safe place for them to tell the truth. Not every world was pretty, but with poetry, poignant and powerful language could be used to convey it.

One student wrote a poem about having eye surgery and how sad he was that his dad wasn't there at the hospital. The student, who was in third grade, began to cry when he read his poem, and the teacher called his mother, who had no idea how he felt about that incident.

Nikki, a second-grader, wrote of her safe haven in a poem:

"My Secret Place I Love"

I have a place where the moon shines so
bright that you do not need a sun.
Whenever I go there I have a spectacular time.
It is where the stars come out in the day.
It is where the trees and roses talk a lot.

Poetry-writing workshops usually ranged from four to eight weeks per classroom, but Kellogg School had year-long residencies that spanned several years, so there was time to teach revision, and three amazing teachers offered to have their classes participate in this process. They were Marti Nichols (second/third grade), Maxine Scott (third grade), and Pat Dreyer (fifth grade).

Each of those teachers was fully committed to poetry. Marti was the one who came up with the concept of "Poetryland." Maxine reported to the principal how students who had participated in poetry-writing workshops the year prior had writing skills superior to those students who had not. Pat encouraged lessons on revision. Another teacher, who taught sixth grade, always wrote with the students and always read her poems. Once, while reading, she began to cry. The students were awestruck to see their teacher so vulnerable and exposed. For them, it was a miracle.

Writing poetry is different from other kinds of writing, and sometimes teachers are surprised to learn that their students with the most advanced language skills are not necessarily their most creative students when it comes to poetry. Often the "troublemaker" or the student who lives quietly in his or her own world produces the most thought-provoking and imaginative poems in the class. Those students learn to use poetry as a tool for survival.

And if students are angry, they need to be encouraged to write about it. The motto is: "Don't punch; write a poem instead." If they say what they feel in words, they don't have to show their poem to anyone. They'll get their feelings out and won't get into trouble. Giving them this permission always brings smiles to their faces.

When it comes to writing with very young students, the visiting poet and/or teacher needs to take dictation, skipping lines, so the students can easily copy the words, or if necessary, trace over them. Group poems work well with four-year-old preschoolers, transitional kindergarten classes (California students whose birthdays are in the fall and who miss the cutoff date to start regular kindergarten), and kindergarten classes, so the experience becomes an oral one where each student contributes a line, and together, the class creates a poem.

When teachers aren't needed to assist with writing, they can write with the students and can read their poem to the class, if they choose. It's actually a rare teacher who reads her or his poem aloud to the class, and it's really magical for the students.

The process doesn't stop here. Once drafts are written, there's always revision. If students are going to embrace the craft of poetry, they need to discover the unfolding world of language and learn to edit their work. In some classrooms, particularly in upper grades, students often work collaboratively on revision.

Before beginning revision, first have the students generate a lot of poetry. Then begin each session by writing a student poem on the whiteboard or projecting it with a document camera. Then have the students revise the poems as a class. Here is a format they can use:

1. The student poet reads the poem aloud.
2. The class acknowledges the strengths of the poem.
3. Students ask questions for clarification.
4. The class goes through the poem line by line, eliminating useless words and clichés, suggesting additions in places where information is sparse, and pointing out strengths as well as things that aren't working or places where the language needs to be tightened.
5. Students make suggestions for changes, such as adding images, similes, or alliteration, and work with the author, allowing her or him to make the actual changes.
6. Students point out spelling and grammatical errors.
7. The student poet reads the poem aloud and the class scans it for natural breath lines.

After completing this revision process, make a copy of the revised poem on the whiteboard next to the original. Or project it onto the board with a document camera. Then have the class go through a checklist, also on the board or a poster, which includes: imagination, five senses, detail, color, imagery, metaphor/simile, rhythm, and form. It's most important to ask the student poet how he or she feels about the revised poem. The answer is almost always positive.

The process doesn't stop after students revise their poems, either. At the end of a long residency, students can receive "Poetic Licenses," which read: "_____ is an honorary poet. This license entitles her or him to write poems on any topic for the rest of his or her life." This is serious business for these young poets, and they treasure the license that they've worked hard for.

In addition to making anthologies and posters or having assemblies, another activity is to set up poetry pen pals with students from different schools.

It doesn't matter what grade they're in. Elementary- and high-school students can even be pen pals with college students. Teachers can also arrange field trips. Students at Fred Williams Elementary School in Port Hueneme, California came to poetry readings at neighboring Oxnard College, for example.

Over the years, students have written thank-you letters to the visiting poet on their own or as a class assignment during the workshops or after they ended. A first-grader, Emily, wrote: "I wish Shelley would teach the whole world poetry." A sixth-grader, Cloe, wrote, "What I found out about myself was that I have an imagination. And a good one." These cards were proof that for students at any age, poetry is a portal to their imaginations and to finding out who they really are.

Sometimes parents also write letters to the visiting poet. Many years ago, Jackie Thomas wrote a card saying, "Thank you for 'awakening' my children to poetry." Her daughter, Heather, loved poetry, but when Jackie spoke at a board meeting at Chula Vista City Schools, she talked about how surprised she was to see the amazing poem her fifth-grade son had written, how she framed it along with one of Heather's poems and gave them to their grandparents for a present.

Some mothers cry when they read their children's poems at open houses or hear them at school assemblies. Poetry becomes a family event, and everyone in that family feels proud. This is just one step along the path that a young student's poem travels.

SAMPLE WRITING EXERCISES

Note: These lessons combine grades pre-K through grade 2 and grades 3 through 5. Each has a full curriculum of eight lessons. Many of the lessons can be interchanged at all of these grade levels.

Part I: Pre-K Through Second Grade

1) Imagination: Imaginary Friends

Ask the students: "Is imagination real or make-believe?" Some say real; some say make-believe. Then have them close their eyes and on the count of three imagine a purple elephant coming into the room. "One, two, three!" They open their eyes, but there's no purple elephant. "But how many people can imagine that?" Hands go up. "So the imagination must be make-believe, and the people who thought so were right."

Then they close their eyes again, and this time imagine that it's recess or lunchtime, and they're all going to leave this room. "One, two, three!" They open their eyes. Tell them that everyone knows that recess and lunch are going to happen, and everyone can certainly imagine that, so the imagination must be real, too, and everyone is right.

Then tell them that they're going to write about an imaginary friend or animal or themselves as an imaginary animal. First read a model poem.

"Self-Portrait as a Bear," by Donald Hall

Here is a fat animal, a bear
that is partly a dodo.
Ridiculous wings hang at his shoulders
while he plods in the brickyards
at the edge of the city, smiling
and eating flowers. He eats them
because he loves them
because they are beautiful
because they love him.
It is eating flowers which makes him fat.
He carries his huge stomach
over the gutters of damp leaves
in the parking lots in October,
but inside that paunch
he knows there are fields of lupine
and meadows of mustard and poppy.
He encloses sunshine.
Winds bend the flowers
in combers across the valley,
birds hang on the stiff wind,
at night there are showers, and the sun
lifts through a haze every morning
of the summer in the stomach.

Now it's time to write. With preschool and sometimes with kindergarten, it's good to do a group poem, where each student makes up a line, and you write it on the board, the document camera, or butcher paper. With first and second grade, you can dismiss the students to their seats in the manner explained in the introduction, and then circulate, helping those students who are stuck and putting stickers on their poems. If they finish early, they can either write more, add a title, or draw a picture if they want.

Then call them back to the rug with their poems. If they're not done writing, ask them to still come to the rug and finish their poems later, unless you feel that it's important for certain students to finish their poems. Many eager students come as soon as they are done. With younger students, almost everyone wants to read, so allow time for this. Call up two students at a time, as explained in the introduction.

Here are some student poems from this lesson.

"Imaginary Friend," by Abigail, first grade

I have an imaginary
friend and no one
knows that, only I
know. And I have
a whole world of
imaginary friends in
my ear and they
are so bad.
They go every place.
They get on books
and they climb
every place.

"Untitled," by Jeremy, second grade

I have an imaginary
dinosaur. He has very
powerful legs.
We ride bikes
together.

2) Five Senses: Creating Your World

Have the students come to the poetry circle and tell them that today you're going to tell them the story of Little Red Riding Hood. But most of them already know that story and are telling it to their younger brothers and sisters. So explain that this is the poetry version of the story. They all know that Little Red Riding Hood had to go to her grandmother's house to deliver a basket of goodies. And to get to her grandma's house, she had to go through the forest. Ask: "How will she know when she gets to the forest?" The answer they usually give is that she'll see the trees.

"Oh, but these mean men came and blindfolded her, so she couldn't see a thing. So there went Little Red Riding Hood and she couldn't see. How will she know when she gets to the forest?" The answer they usually give is that she can feel the trees with her hands. Tell them that if she could feel, then she'd take off the blindfold. "The mean men thought about that and tied her hands behind her back. So she couldn't see or feel. How will she know when she gets to the forest?" The answer they usually give is that she can hear. "What will she hear?" They name birds, small animals, and so on.

Then you explain that it was very cold that day, so Little Red Riding Hood's mother made her wear very thick earmuffs, so she couldn't hear anything. "How will she know when she gets to the forest?" The answer this time is that she can smell the trees and flowers. "That's true. But Little Red Riding Hood had a terrible cold, and she couldn't smell a thing. So how will she know when she gets to the forest?" They say she can still taste. "What can she taste?" They list berries and other fruit. "But if her nose is stuffed from a cold, she probably can't taste, either," you explain.

The moral of the story is: "You don't go to Grandma's house when you have a cold. No, just kidding." Explain that the wolf teaches Little Red Riding Hood a lesson on how to use her five senses because when she sees him, she says: "Grandma, what big eyes you have!" And he answers: "The better to see you with." The conversation continues: "Grandma, what big hands you have!" "The better to feel you with." Proceed through the five senses with the students chanting: "The better to ___ you with."

After you establish the importance of using the five senses, talk about how students can create their own make-believe worlds using their five senses. Tell the students to imagine a world somewhere else and ask them what they would put into that world. There's a wonderful Australian picture book called *Dunbi the Owl*, written by Daisy Utemorrah, published by Mad Hatter Books (ISBN: 0-915391-07-4), which is available on Amazon.com. It's a creation story with a great moral and uses the five senses. Also read a model poem.

"One More October," by Amy Uyematsu

I walk
slower
now

bow
in the yellow
of falling
leaves

I come
from
a sunlit world

born
to rise up
then
let go

Point out how the sense of sight and touch are used here and talk about how the poet creates a world outside, where she comes from. Then students return to their seats and write poems creating a world using some of their five senses. It can be a make-believe world or a real world. There could be orange popsicles falling from the sky or candy growing on pink trees—whatever they want. They're in charge.

Here are some student poems from this lesson.

"How the World Began," by Emmanuel, second grade

The world began with dinosaurs
and swamps and little creatures crawling
in the deadly swamps with big trees.
Then they died. After came man,
the first one who knew about the circle.

"The Most Amazing Thing I Ever Saw," by Brett, second grade

right there when the world
was just getting started
I saw mountains coming up

they were sprouting like plants
some were big some were
small and fat

the first two people were
made out of earth
or you can call it dirt
at this time

I saw animals too
I named some hawks
some goats some
sharks some
leprechauns

some plants like grass
poison ivy
apple tree and
pear tree
and the ocean
then the desert with
hills that were big
and small

3) Detail: Becoming Very Small

Talk about the importance of using details in poems. Then tell the students that one way they can notice details is to zoom into something very small, like crawling inside a flower or a seashell or a stone. A whole world exists inside there, and sometimes they need to use their imaginations to see that world. Then read a model poem about going inside a stone and imagining what's there.

"Stone," by Charles Simic

Go inside a stone
That would be my way.
Let somebody else become a dove
Or gnash with a tiger's tooth.
I am happy to be a stone.

From the outside the stone is a riddle:
No one knows how to answer it.
Yet within, it must be cool and quiet
Even though a cow steps on it full weight,
Even though a child throws it in a river;
The stone sinks, slow, unperturbed
To the river bottom
Where the fishes come to knock on it
And listen.

I have seen sparks fly out
When two stones are rubbed,
So perhaps it is not dark inside after all;
Perhaps there is a moon shining
From somewhere, as though behind a hill—
Just enough light to make out
The strange writings, the star-charts
On the inner walls.

Talk about how it could be possible to have a world inside a stone with a moon shining and star charts. Then ask them to pretend that they are very, very small and can climb inside a stone or rock and to write a poem about what's inside there. Remind them to use as much detail as possible.

Here are some student poems from this lesson.

"Being a Rock," by Christie, second grade

You have to be quiet.
You have to be a good swimmer.
Or else if someone throws
you in the water and forgets you,
you will be stuck. And please
believe me, I've been there.

"The Moon Cheetah," by Alyssa, second grade

Inside my rock there is
a moon cheetah. The moon
cheetah is furry   it is smelling
something sweet   it hears some
thing squeal   it is my
hamster. The moon cheetah
feels something sticky   it
is goo   it's on the floor because
we set a trap for the moon
cheetah.

4) Color: What Colors Make Me Feel or Remind Me Of

Start by saying, "Let's imagine the classroom without color. Everything is black and white. That would not be an interesting world." Then read a model poem that uses lots of colors, but first explain that it's about a hermit. Ask if they know what a hermit is, and they'll usually say it's a crab that lives in a shell. Explain that they are right. "That's a hermit crab. But a hermit *person* is someone who likes to be alone and usually lives alone." Here is the poem.

"The Hermit Picks Berries," by Maxine Kumin

At midday the birds doze.
So does he.

The frogs cover themselves.
So does he.

The breeze holds its breath in the poplars.
Not one leaf turns its back.
He admires the stillness.

The snake uncoils its clay self
in the sun on a rock in the pasture.
It is the hermit's pasture.
He encourages the snake.

At this hour a goodly number
of blueberries decide to ripen.
Once they were wax white.
Then came the green of small bruises.
After that, the red of bad welts.
All this time they enlarged themselves.
Now they are true blue.

The hermit whistles as he picks.
Later he will put on his shirt
and walk to town for some cream.

Point out how the poem uses colors to describe the ripening of the berries: "wax white" and "the green of small bruises" and "the red of bad welts" and "true blue." The poem is a portrait of a hermit, a man who likes to be by himself, who goes out into a pasture to pick berries. He whistles all the while, shirtless, because "later he will put on his shirt/ and walk to town for some cream." And they can all imagine the taste of blueberries and cream.

Tell them that they are going to write poems about colors, and they can write how the colors make them feel, or they can describe the colors. This time dismiss them to their seats differently. Bring out a box of crayons with unusual names for the colors, like "robin's nest blue," or "purple mountain majesty," or "macaroni and cheese," or "mauvelous," or "tickle me pink."

Give each of them a crayon that you chose *especially* for that person and suggest that the students write the name of the color as the title of their poem. But they can't use the crayon to write with. Excited, they go back to their seats and begin writing. If they don't like their color, which seldom happens, they can write about how nasty it is, or they can write about any color they want.

Here are some student poems from this lesson. Interestingly, one of the students chose to write about white.

"White," by Tera, second grade

White like the snow
falling on your head
and the bright stars
that twinkle at night.
White like the milk
I drink. White is so many
happy things, but I'm
so glad that I don't
have a white heart.

"Midnight Blue," by Juan, second grade

Midnight Blue, the color of midnight, dark
jeans of a 32-year-old man
slithering along the ground. He is a thief.
The color of a ninja
on the underside of my skateboard.
Ice, at the Arctic Ocean. The darkest
shade of blue I've ever seen.

5) Feelings: When I'm Happy, Sad, or Scared

Make a list on the board of all of the feelings a person can experience. Ask, "If you were going to Disneyland, how would you feel?" They say "excited."

Then ask, "If your cat died, how would we feel?" Of course, the answer is "sad."

Then give them another example: *It's dark and raining outside. Your mom went to the store to get something, and you're all alone. Suddenly, the lights go out and the shutters bang. Then there's a knock on the door.* Everyone knows that you're scared, but you never said the word. Tell them, "That's how you want to *show* that you are scared." Then read a model poem expressing a certain feeling.

"Moon Tiger," by Denise Levertov

The moon tiger.
in the room, here.
It came in, it is
prowling sleekly
under and over
the twin beds.
See its small head,
silver smooth,
hear the pad of its
large feet. Look,
its white stripes
in the light that slid
through the jalousies.
It is sniffing our
clothes, its cold nose
nudges our bodies.
The beds are narrow,
but I'm coming in with you.

Explain that jalousies are shutters or blinds, then ask them what the moon tiger is. You will get all kinds of answers, but tell them to imagine having blinds on the windows and a pile of clothes on the floor or a chair. If there's a full moon out, and the light shines through the blinds in the dark, it might cast a shadow on the clothes that looks like a moon. And the blinds might look like stripes.

Then ask how the person in the poem was feeling, and they all say, "scared." But the poet didn't say she was scared, "so how did you know this?" Talk about how the poem describes how the speaker experiences the moon tiger with her five senses and then crawls into bed with someone else, so she or he must feel scared.

Tell them to recreate an experience in their poems that made them feel a certain way, so that everyone knows what they are feeling without their having to say it. When they read their poems, ask the students what the person in the poem was feeling or how they felt when they heard the poem. Of course, some students will still name a feeling, and that's okay.

Here are some student poems. The first one mentions being mad, but the speaker really feels deep sadness. The second poem is titled "Sadness," but the speaker is really scared.

"Shot in the Head," by Deanna, second grade

I cuddle with him,
my dog,
when I'm mad at my dad
for dying.

"Sadness," by Maria, first grade

In the darkness
a white coat
moving in the
closet. Someone was
there, I don't
know who, but the
sadness was in my
heart.

6) Images: What Lives in the Sky and Dreams

Write the word "image" on the board and tell students, "An image is a picture made out of words." Everyone says it together. Then they say it in a very high voice, then in a very low voice, then in a very loud voice and finally, in a very soft voice, almost a whisper: "An image is a picture made out of words."

By now, they will remember what an image is. "And when is the imagination having the most fun making up images?" Eventually, you will get the answer, "When we are sleeping and dreaming." Then ask them to name things that live in the sky. You don't mean birds, which fly up into the sky, but things like clouds or rain or the sun. Then read a model poem.

from "Six Significant Landscapes," by Wallace Stevens

IV
When my dream was near the moon,
The white folds of its gown
Filled with yellow light.
The soles of its feet
Grew red.
Its hair filled
With certain blue crystallizations
From stars,
Not far off.

Talk about the image of the moon in the dream, wearing a white gown, and having red feet and blue hair. Ask the students again to name other things that live in the sky, but this time to imagine what they dream about. That's what they will write about. Put on the board, "The _____ dreams about," and they can use that for their first line, if they want to.

Here are some student poems from this assignment.

"Untitled," by Adam, first grade

The whole sky dreams about
swallowing me and drinking
the Milky Way.

"The Sun," by Vanessa, second grade

The sun dreams of more fire.
The sun dreams of seeing the night
and talking with the stars.
The sun dreams of tagging the moon.
The sun and the moon play tag
running around the earth.

7) Similes: Monsters in "Monsterland" and Other Scary Creatures

Talk about what a simile is and practice making them, as follows: ask students to describe the tree on the playground. Someone says it's tall. Ask, "As tall as what?" The response is: "The tree is as tall as a giant." Then continue making up other similes using the tree and then other things. Ask them to smile their biggest smile and show their similes.

Next talk about monsters and other scary creatures. Tell students that they're going to write about monsters using similes, and they're going to make the similes unusual. For example, they could write, "My monster is as white as lightning." Also, they can make friends with the scary creature if they want to. They can feed it milk and cookies, watch TV with it, or go rollerblading together. You want them to use their imaginations. Then read a short model poem.

"A Late Spring Day in My Life," by Robert Bly

A silence hovers over the earth:
The grass lifts lightly in the heat
Like the ancient wing of a bird.
A horse gazes steadily at me.

Talk about what "ancient" means and tell them that long, long ago, birds were very, very big and were scary, like monsters. Then reread the simile emphasizing the word "like": "The grass lifts lightly in the heat/ *like* the ancient wing of a bird." Ask students to write a poem about a monster, a good one or a bad one, and to use a simile to describe it. Not everyone will write similes, so find other things that are working well in the poem to respond to, for example, how the speaker felt about the monster.

Here are some student poems from this assignment. The first one doesn't use similes, but the second one does.

"Untitled," by Tiffany, first grade

I had a monster in my
closet. He did not have
teeth, but he died.
My monster died.

"Dragons," by Jason, second grade

There are dragons in my room.
One is golden and it blows its nose.
A red dragon makes fire
and one dragon blows my dreams away.
One dragon is shiny like a rainbow
and one dragon shines like silver.
I always dream about dragons.

8) Rhythm: Magic

Talk about different ways to put rhythm into poems, like repeating words or phrases or having long or short lines. Then talk about magic. Sometimes magic spells or chants repeat certain words and have a rhythm. Then read a model poem that has a lot of repetition and also some rhyme, but focus on the rhythm, not the rhyme.

"The Magical Mouse," by Kenneth Patchen

I am the magical mouse
I don't eat cheese
I eat sunsets
And tops of trees

I don't wear fur

I wear funnels
Of lost ships and the weather
That's under dead leaves
I am the magical mouse

I don't fear cats

Or woodowls
I do as I please
Always
I don't eat crusts
I am the magical mouse
I eat
Little birds and maidens

That taste like dust

Talk about how the poet created a rhythm by repeating "I don't" and "I am a magical mouse." Then tell the students to write poems about something magical. It could be a magic animal or something they pretend to do that's magical, like becoming invisible and peeking in on people or flying or turning into a monkey.

Here are some student poems from this exercise.

"Magic," by Toni, second grade

To make a giraffe fly,
you have to get wings from the store.
You have to put them on the giraffe,
and throw it up in the air.
When you want to make a donkey sing,
you teach it words,
then you teach it a song.
The world is full of magic,
you just have to see.

"Red Rat," by Shannon, first grade

I have a magic animal
who sweeps the stars
out of the sky.

I have a magic animal
who eats pretty
little flowers and
bad little mice.

I have a magic animal.

Sample Writing Exercises—Part II: Third Through Fifth Grade

1) Imagination: What America Is Like to You

Today, students are going to use their imaginations to write poems. They are going to imagine what America is like for them and write about that. Ask them: "What's in your world? What do you do every day? What do you see when you walk down the street?" They might say soccer practice, homework, and so on. Then read a model poem by a famous poet, Walt Whitman. Tell them that his poetry is taught in college classes, and when they get to college, they can say they learned his poetry in third, fourth, or fifth grade. Walk around the room as you read.

"I Hear America Singing," by Walt Whitman

I HEAR America singing, the varied carols I hear,
Those of mechanics, each one singing his as it should be blithe and strong,
The carpenter singing his as he measures his plank or beam,
The mason singing his as he makes ready for work, or leaves off work,
The boatman singing what belongs to him in his boat, the deckhand singing on the steamboat deck,
The shoemaker singing as he sits on his bench, the hatter singing as he stands,
The wood-cutter's song, the ploughboy's on his way in the morning, or at noon intermission or at sundown,
The delicious singing of the mother, or of the young wife at work, or of the girl sewing or washing,
Each singing what belongs to him or her and to none else,
The day what belongs to the day—at night the party of young fellows, robust, friendly,
Singing with open mouths their strong melodious songs.

Talk about all the things that people do in the poem to make America happen, like the carpenters, hatmakers, shoemakers, and sewing girls—all working and singing. Then tell them to write a poem about their world, what America is like for them, what they see and what they do. Encourage them to use their imaginations when picturing their world.

Here are two student poems from this exercise—very different poems, both observing what they see in their America.

"Untitled," by Shane, fourth grade

America is like a wave
hitting the shore.
Crabs walking
up rocks and whales hitting
boats so hard they
flip over.
Boats crying for
help at sea.
People swimming
sharks eating fish

and sleeping.
Clocks waking up
people in their
boats.

That is what
the world is like
to me.

"America 1987," by Jack, fourth grade

America,
microwave ovens
with money for
nothin', but you have
to earn it.

'87 is skateboards,
surfing,
wasted resources—
like rotten
apples.

Tough dreams of power.

2) Five Senses: Sounds, Sights, Tastes, Smells, Touch of Darkness

Ask: "Who's hungry?" Tell the students that you're going to bring in pizza. Everyone gets excited. Say that you're going to set it down and they're going to listen to the pizza. No one gets it. Then say that you're going to bring in hip hop music. Everyone gets excited. Then tell them they're going to smell the hip hop music. "But that doesn't make sense," they say.

Then tell them that you're going to bring in a bouquet of fragrant flowers, and they're going to watch the flowers. They shake their heads because there must be something wrong. Then you're going to bring in a great popular movie, like *Batman*, and they're going to feel the movie. "That can't be right," they say. Tell them you're going to bring in cuddly Teddy bears, and they're going to taste the stuffed animals. "You must be confused," they say. Finally, you ask: "What did I mix up?" They know—your five senses!

Ask: "Why are your five senses so important?" Then tell them the next time they have pizza in the cafeteria, to eat it really slowly, to chew in slow motion and *taste* the pizza, rather than swallowing it hot. Tell them that when all the other kids are done with their pizza, they'll be jealous because you'll still have some.

After that discussion, announce that you're giving them homework. Everyone groans. It's Friday, and they don't get homework on Fridays. "Oh, but this is poetry homework. It's different," you say. They just have to do the assignment and verbally report back on Monday. Here it is:

Go home, and when you walk through the door, hug the first person you see (not your dog). Your mom will love this. Open the refrigerator and get out a healthy snack and eat it—not chips or candy! Turn on some music for just a few minutes and listen to it carefully. But don't blast your grandma! Then go outside and smell something growing in your yard or a park nearby, such as grass or a flower or a tree.

Sit down on the grass and feel it. While you're sitting there, look around and notice something that you didn't see before—not a brand new plant—but something that's been there for a long time that you just didn't notice was there. That's it.

They all agree that it will be the most fun homework they've ever gotten, especially on a Friday. Tell them that today they're going to write poems using at least two or three of their five senses. Explain that they should not just list their senses, but rather incorporate them into their poems. Then read a model poem.

"Crossing Place," by W. S. Merwin

I crossed the stream
on the rocks
in the summer
evening
trying not to spill
the pitcher of water
from the falls

When you read this poem, students can hear the sound of the water as night is coming on. It's not just a drizzling sound, but a gush of water, as the poet describes "the pitcher of water/from the falls." Ask them to think to themselves, not out loud, what sounds or lack of sounds they hear at night and begin their poems from there. They can also add in some of the other five senses.

Here are two student poems using a few of the five senses.

"Silent Night," by Maria, fourth grade

The air is cold on this silent night.
Dark lurks in every corner.
Big buildings lean
like goblins haunting the moon.

The still river sleeps quietly.
Trees wait for morning light.
And everything is silent,
silent like a midnight ghost.

"Right Back Home," by Jonathan, fourth grade

We were out in the dark
at dusk with the wind
when the moon snapped in half
and fell on our car
when half rolled away
with the wind howling loud
with a crash and a thud
and a smooth but big splash.
The other half went down.
I saw all the fish
and a shark with a fin.
We went down so deep
there wasn't a sound.
We swam up real fast
and took a breath for our lives
and walked back home
slow and quiet.

3) Detail and Alliteration: Going on an Adventure

Ask if anyone has ever been to an art museum. Many students have gone on a class field trip to an art museum at least once. If not, everyone has seen paintings before. Ask if they ever saw a painting with a woman seated, wearing a beautiful dress—maybe purple or red or royal blue. Most of them will nod. From far away, they can see the folds of the dress—the wrinkles. But when they get up close, they just see some lines in black. Those lines make the wrinkles.

Then have them imagine looking at a shirt that lies flat on their bed, all smooth. If they put it on, what do they get? Wrinkles. So when artists want to paint those wrinkles, they have to use darker shades of that color and sometimes black. Those are very important details. The students also need to get those kinds of details into their poems for them to come alive; they have to put in the wrinkles. When they are doing this, they can also pay attention to sounds, particularly repetition of consonant sounds, which is alliteration.

Tell them that today they're going on adventures in their imaginations, and they're going to write about it with lots of rich details in their poems. Ask what kinds of adventures they've been on. Some have gone camping or visited their grandparents in other states or in Mexico. Others went to Disneyland. Tell them it can be an adventure just going outside onto the playground where there are lots of details.

Then read a model poem that was written a long time ago, so it rhymes. Tell students to pay attention to the details in the poem. There's a wonderful edition illustrated by Susan Jeffers and published by E.P. Dutton (ISBN: 0-525-40115-6), so if you happen to get a copy of it, read from that, holding up the pictures as you circulate.

"Stopping by Woods on a Snowy Evening," by Robert Frost

Whose woods these are I think I know.
His house is in the village though;
He will not see me stopping here
To watch his woods fill up with snow.

My little horse must think it queer
To stop without a farmhouse near
Between the woods and frozen lake
The darkest evening of the year.

He gives his harness bells a shake
To ask if there is some mistake.
The only other sound's the sweep
Of easy wind and downy flake.

The woods are lovely, dark and deep.
But I have promises to keep,
And miles to go before I sleep,
And miles to go before I sleep.

Ask what details they heard in the poem. They may notice "the sweep/ Of easy wind and downy flake." That description tells them that it's not a blizzard, but just light snow falling. There is also the detail of the horse that "gives his harness bells a shake." And there is alliteration in the poem, as well, with the repetition of the consonant "d," in "dark and deep" and "s" in "The only other sound's the sweep."

Now it's time to write, and students are to go on an adventure in their imaginations and write, using as much detail as they can. It can be a memory of a place they've been to or a make-believe adventure.

Here are two student poems from this assignment. The first poem has wonderful details, such as: "The sky falls into my hands and the wilderness is mine." The second poem uses great alliteration in the first line repeating the sound of "b": "Biking is like balancing a book on a bumpy/ sidewalk."

"Wilderness," by Ashley, fourth grade

Flashing colors, dripping sweat, burning desire.
I stop.
A swift breeze cools me
and the smell of wild pine and pollen urges me on.
The sky falls into my hands and the wilderness is mine.
The murmur of a tiny creek
calls me to the wild mountain forests.
A gusty wind sends wool clouds whirling by.
The afternoon sun lingers behind the grassy hills.
A blanket of darkness closes a door
as night arrives.

"Biking," by Cameron, fourth grade

Biking is like balancing a book on a bumpy
sidewalk. But when you get going
the wind runs as fast as water
to keep up with you.
You keep on going, soon you're speeding.
You jump off the ramp.
Flying like a bird, you come in for a landing.
You are still going as fast as a cheetah,
but this time the wind stops and pants.

4) Color and Figurative Language

First talk about the importance of putting color in their poems to make them come more alive. Then explain the concept of figurative language. It includes personification, metaphors, and similes. Personification is giving human characteristics to something that isn't human. For example, "If a tree could talk, what would it say? If a chair could walk on its legs and follow you around the room, what would that experience be like?"

Then talk about similes. Give them the example, "His hair is as white as winter." You're comparing his hair to winter. It helps to put the color in the line, so they can imagine it. Ask them to give you other examples of similes using their hair, then eyes, then the grass, and so on. Explain that metaphors do the same thing, only they don't use the word "like" or "as," so you would say, "His hair *is* white winter."

Read a model poem that uses a metaphor, a simile and personification.

"The Boat," by Peter Levitt

> *I turn away from the moon*
> *and hear nightfish knocking against the bow.*
> —Meng Haoran

Morning is a ghost
as it moves
    through its dream,
mountain apes howling
back and forth to one another,
tossing insults like perfect
smooth stones
    that fall
and clatter on the walls
of this canyon,
    into ravines.
There is no way to rise
into the day,
    through the quiet
shattering of light, which
scatters the pattern
of leaves
    onto the surface
of this lake. There
is no way to quiet
these apes,
    who fear the moon,
its darkness. Down,
against the wooden bow
of this boat, nightfish
are knocking. They will continue,
the small constant thud
of their bodies a reminder
as I tear upwards
    through this mist
which gathers its skin
around me as I sleep.

O Moon, fruit of the night tree
& the night. Moon who is no different.
Dark lover of earth. Crescent moon.

Light whose body is the vessel,
and the tide. Here,
with your eye on my naked body,
is one old man
   in a boat, rowing.

Talk about how the poem, as a whole, is a giant metaphor that equates sleep to a man rowing his boat in the morning moonlight. The poem begins with the metaphor, "Morning is a ghost" and adds the simile, "tossing insults like perfect/ smooth stones."

There are also three examples of personification. The first is in the lines, "against the wooden bow/ of this boat nightfish/ are knocking. They will continue." Everyone knows that fish can't really knock. Only humans can do that. The second example is in the lines, "Through this mist/ which gathers its skin." Again, everyone knows that mist doesn't have skin; people do. The third example refers to the moon as a person, the "Dark lover of earth. Crescent moon."

The poet managed to get a metaphor, a simile, and personification into his poem. That's a tall order, and you don't expect anyone else to do all that. Even though he doesn't use color, encourage students to write a poem that focuses on a color, in addition to figurative language. It can be an ordinary color, a boring color, or an unusual color. They can describe the color or give the color a life, if they want to. They can use personification and make it into a person and use metaphors and similes, if they want to.

Here are two student poems. The first uses personification and the second uses metaphors and similes. They both use color.

"Columbine," by Flavio, fifth grade

Columbine, so tender and warm
sleeping in nature's voice
calling for her friends to come
shaping into a star
running so softly with her yellow mouth
rolling its petals so red
running and walking at the same time
running from nature's violence
scratching the walls with her vines
opening the door to her home
and realizing she's safe and sound.

"Gray," by Isaac, fourth grade

Gray is a blur,
the color of an alley trash can,
the sound of destruction itself
or a boxer punching on a punching bag.
On the other side
it is calm.
It's like a river
then a waterfall
coming from clouds of heaven.
Gray is like a clay kind of goo
or slime of a monster
coming in an outrage of speed.
Or it is a crack
in the sidewalk,
a middle of a fog
that never goes away,
the center of the sun,
piping hot.
You never see it.
It is a very boring
color of gray.
Gray is so soft.

5) Feelings and Persona: Show and Recreate Experiences—Don't *Tell*

Begin by telling the students a story about what happened yesterday: *I was playing catch with my dog in the front yard. I threw the ball too far and it went into the street. My dog ran after it, and all of a sudden I saw a car coming and yelled, "Stop!" But I was too late. The car hit my dog. I ran into the street where my dog was lying. He licked my hand, then closed his eyes forever.*

The room is silent. One kid gasps. Some kids have tears in their eyes. Pause with the silence, then say, "That didn't really happen. I don't even have a dog." But you make a point when you ask the students what you were feeling. They say, "sad." Ask what *they* were feeling when you told the story. They say, "sad." But you never used the word "sad" in your story. The description *told* them that you were sad.

Today, they're going to focus on expressing their feelings in poems without stating the actual word, such as "happy" or "sad." If they want, they can recreate any experience that made them feel a certain way—without stating that feeling. It can be a sad feeling of a loss or a happy or excited feeling or an angry feeling.

Then explain the concept of persona, writing from someone else's point of view, as if they actually were that person. Read a model poem that expresses a strong emotion of sadness and loss of a friendship. The poem is in the voice of a girl who was going to a Japanese internment camp during World War II.

Before you read the poem, explain to those who don't know that during that time, the United States was at war with Germany and Japan, and the U.S. government made the Japanese people living in this country move out of their homes and into a kind of prison camp. The government did it out of fear, but it was the wrong thing to do. Everyone knows now that it's wrong to pick on someone just because of his or her race. Here's the poem.

"IN RESPONSE TO EXECUTIVE ORDER 9066: All Americans of Japanese Descent Must Report to Relocation Centers," by Dwight Okita

Dear Sirs:
Of course I'll come. I've packed my galoshes
and three packets of tomato seeds. Denise calls them
love apples. My father says where we're going
they won't grow.

I am a fourteen-year-old girl with bad spelling
and a messy room. If it helps any, I will tell you
I have always felt funny using chopsticks
and my favorite food is hot dogs.
My best friend is a white girl named Denise—
we look at boys together. She sat in front of me
all through grade school because of our names:
O'Connor, Ozawa. I know the back of Denise's head very well.
I tell her she's going bald. She tells me I copy on tests.
We are best friends.

I saw Denise today in Geography class.
She was sitting on the other side of the room.
"You're trying to start a war," she said, "giving secrets
away to the Enemy, Why can't you keep your big
mouth shut?"

I didn't know what to say.
I gave her a packet of tomato seeds
and asked her to plant them for me, told her
when the first tomato ripened
she'd miss me.

Talk about how the speaker in this poem felt; everyone agrees that she was "sad," even though she didn't say the word. Then point out that the poem was written by a man, but the speaker is a girl. That makes it a persona poem. After hearing the poem, students can grasp that concept fairly easily.

Now it's time to write a poem that expresses an emotion and allows that feeling to come through in the poem without stating it. Students can write a persona poem if they want to, but they don't have to. Here are two student poems that are not written in personas, but capture deep feelings of loss.

"I Lost," by Jacob, fourth grade

I lost my birth dad.
He died in a car crash.
It's such a sad feeling.
He went through the
windshield and onto the street.
His name was Richard Tostada.
I wish he'd never died.
We could be fishing.

"Feeding My Rabbits," by Beau, fifth grade

1st year
In summer when it's warm I feed my fourteen rabbits.
The green food pellets falling into the bowl like Cheerios,
the green water bucket full of water
so full, so heavy, splashing out on the way.

2nd year
Fall diseases come and seven rabbits die.
They lie there like stale donuts.

3rd year
Winter is when the water freezes over
and the food turns hard.
It is also when four rabbits freeze to death.

5th year
Spring is when the food store
loses our business.
My parents get a divorce and my dog dies.
Three left. We sell the rabbits and their cages, too.

6) Imagery: Dreams

Write the word "image" on the board, and before you can finish writing the word, someone shouts out, "imagination." So write the word "imagination" on the board and show them how the word "image" comes right out of "imagination" and that students use their imaginations to create images. Explain that they can create pictures by making vivid images. In fact, they can create motion pictures, so someone from Hollywood could come in and make a movie out of their poem because the images are so clear and unique. They like that idea.

Ask them the same question you would ask younger students: "When does the imagination have the most fun making up images?" The answer is the same: "When you're sleeping and dreaming." Dreams give us all kinds of unique and strange images. They can be happy or sad or scary nightmares. They can be weird, like someone comes to school and the teacher is in her or his pajamas. Or maybe it's his or her grandmother teaching the class. Those things happen in dreams.

Then ask how many people have had dreams of falling or flying or trying to get somewhere they couldn't get to. Ask if they've had good dreams when they wake up and try to go back to sleep and continue the dream. Ask how many of them have had nightmares and wind up in someone else's bed. By now they are all excited about their dreams. Then read a model poem about taking tests. It's a bad dream.

"Pass/Fail," by Linda Pastan

> "Examination dreams are reported to persist even into old age. . . ."
>
> —*Time* magazine

You will never graduate
from this dream
of blue books.
No matter how
you succeed awake,
asleep there is a test
waiting to be failed.
The dream beckons
with two dull pencils,
but you haven't even
taken the course;
when you reach for a book—
it closes a door
in your face; when
you conjugate a verb—
it is in the wrong
language.
Now the pillow becomes

a blank page. Turn it
to the cool side;
you will still smother
in all of the feathers
that have to be learned
by heart.

Explain that blue books are used in college when people take tests. A lot of students can relate to the stress of taking tests. Then ask them to write a poem with images about a dream that they had—a good one, a bad one, a weird one—whatever they want. If they can't remember all of the dream, they can make up new details. And if they can't remember any dream at all, they can invent one. You can even give them one of your bad dreams to write about if they want to. Remind them again to use images—unusual language in their poems.

Here are two student poems about dreams.

"The Plumber," by Talia, third grade

Raggedy boots,
torn shirt
and old jeans.
As I go
out to skip
rope the plumber
comes and starts running
toward me.
I run like lightning
striking a piece
of glass.
The plumber chases
me around the block.
When I stop to
catch my breath
he slows down and
takes his
wrench out
of my pocket
and with it opens
up my dream.

"In the Dark," by Jenny, fourth grade

In the night a small white
light is in my room. I follow it

but out of it comes a large
goblin trying to eat my brain.
I yell, "mommy, help me. There's
a goblin in my room trying
to eat my brain." Then my mom
turns on the light and I say it
is gone. My mom says, "What is gone?"
I say, "the goblin."
The next night I dream I am chased
by a book trying to lock me in
his pages. Then suddenly a big shadow
is following me. Of course I am in
the book pages.
I am in a page where a girl is sleeping
so I fall asleep with her.

7) Rhythm: The Rhythm of War

Ask several students to come to the front of the class. They have no idea why you've chosen them. Ask the class, "What do those students have in common?" After the guessing game, someone in the class figures out that some people are wearing striped or plaid shirts, and some have designs on their clothes. That's right! Point out that they are *all* wearing rhythm. Some of their clothes have predictable patterns, like striped and plaid shirts. Explain that that's what poetry was like long ago. Everyone knew how and when the pattern would repeat.

Then look at the unpredictable patterns. They can see the patterns repeat, but they don't know when or where they will repeat. That's what free verse is like. They might find repetition, but they never know when it will occur. The students go back to their seats, and everyone looks around the room for patterns that are predictable and patterns that are not.

Then talk about war poems. Students live in a world where war is ever present. Fortunately, they don't have a war going on in this country, but some kids are not that lucky. A lot of young people live in a world where war is all around them, and the students can only imagine that. Sometimes they read about it or watch movies about it, but still, they can only imagine it. Sometimes they get into fights with their friends or they see family members fighting, and that's like a mini-war, too.

One thing they need to know is that during wartime, some people write poems. It's a way to express their feelings. For example, the *Star Spangled Banner* was written during war. Read the following model poem, which was written during the Vietnam War.

"Facing It," by Yusef Komunyakaa

My black face fades,
hiding inside the black granite.
I said I wouldn't,
dammit: No tears.
I'm stone. I'm flesh.
My clouded reflection eyes me
like a bird of prey, the profile of night
slanted against morning. I turn
this way—the stone lets me go.
I turn that way—I'm inside
the Vietnam Veterans Memorial
again, depending on the light
to make a difference.
I go down the 58,022 names,
half-expecting to find
my own in letters like smoke.
I touch the name Andrew Johnson;
I see the booby trap's white flash.
Names shimmer on a woman's blouse
but when she walks away
the names stay on the wall.
Brushstrokes flash, a red bird's
wings cutting across my stare.
The sky. A plane in the sky.
A white vet's image floats
closer to me, then his pale eyes
look through mine. I'm a window.
He's lost his right arm
inside the stone. In the black mirror
a woman's trying to erase names:
No, she's brushing a boy's hair.

Talk about the feelings expressed in this poem and how sad the poem is. The speaker has to face the truth about what happened during the Viet Nam War. He is a veteran and is having Posttraumatic Stress Disorder symptoms. He can't decide if he's alive ("flesh") or dead ("stone") because he feels such a personal loss from the war. The speaker remembers the flashbacks of "the booby trap's white flash" and "A white vet's image floats/ closer to me, then his pale eyes/ look through mine. . . ."

Also talk about the Vietnam Memorial, which is a huge piece of granite with names of those who died in that war written on it. Point out the rhythm in the repetition of the lines, "I turn/ this way – the stone lets me go./ I turn that way— . . ." and "The sky. A plane in the sky."

Then tell the students to write a poem about war as they imagine it to be or as they heard about it from a family member. Or they can write about a fight they were once in or witnessed. But their poem should have rhythm. They can repeat words or lines or have very short, skinny lines, so that their poem moves very fast.

Here are two student poems with rhythm.

"Why Is There War?" by Clay, fifth grade

Count every missile you can,
every bullet they make and every gun
they use, every plane that bombs,
every tank that shoots,
every grenade that's tossed,
every body found dead.
Every heart broken.
Now look all around. Is this
a success or a failure?

Count every missile you can, every bullet
they make . . .

"War," by Bobby, fifth grade

The sharp, tall stem
of the bull grass cutting his leg.
But what could be more
foolish like a 3-year-old child?
Ambush.
The sound of gunfire
cracks at the ear.
The bombs bursting
like the anger of the devil.
The force, the powerful
force.
No hope. You have to
think clearly. Emptiness.
You run.
But, all is dark.
A sharp pain in your neck.
You fall like the titanic.
No hope. Words. Names.
50,000 names.
The wall is full. No more
room. It is a packed
car, leaving the earth.

8) Form: Epigraphs

Talk about how poetry has an actual form. This is something that students have been working on for a while. But now it's time for them to be conscious of making their poems *look* like poems, not stories. Tell them that the most important thing is to get their thoughts and feelings out—which is more important than worrying about form right away. But then they can go back and scan the poem for natural breath lines.

Put a few poetry lines on the board that look like prose and have someone read them. Then put in the slashes whenever that student takes a breath. Copy the lines in poetry form on the board next to the original, so everyone can see how the lines now look like a poem. Also remind them that poems are written in stanzas. When they get a new idea, they just skip a line.

Then introduce the concept of epigraphs. Write the word on the board. Explain that it's a quote from another poem, story, or newspaper article that they put in quotation marks or italics under the title of their poem. It relates to the poem and inspires it.

Or they can use the quote as the title of their poem or as the first line. The important thing is to give credit to the author or poet. Demonstrate this by making up a title and writing it on the board. Then take a quote from a poem and write it underneath, indented and in quotation marks or italics. Write a dash and put that author's name on the next line and then skip a space and make up a first line. It might look like this:

My Bones

"My broken arms heal themselves around you."
—Galway Kinnell

When I was nine I fell off the car and broke my arm.
. . . and so on.

Then read a few sections of a very long model poem that has powerful lines that students will use as epigraphs. The poem is about a baby daughter who has a nightmare. The speaker comes into her room, lifts her out of her crib, and imagines all the things he would do for her.

from **"Little Sleep's-Head Sprouting Hair in the Moonlight,"
by Galway Kinnell**

1

You scream, waking from a nightmare.

When I sleepwalk
into your room, and pick you up,

and hold you up in the moonlight, you cling to me
hard,
as if clinging could save us. I think
you think
I will never die, I think I exude
to you the permanence of smoke or stars,
even as
my broken arms heal themselves around you.

2

I have heard you tell
the sun, *don't go down*, I have stood by
as you told the flower, *don't grow old*,
don't die. Little Maud,

I would blow the flame out of your silver cup,
I would suck the rot from your fingernail,
I would brush your sprouting hair of the dying light,
I would scrape the rust off your ivory bones,
I would help death escape through the little ribs of your body,
I would alchemize the ashes of your cradle back into wood,
I would let nothing of you go, ever,

until washerwomen
feel the clothes fall asleep in their hands,
and hens scratch their spell across hatchet blades,
and rats walk away from the cultures of the plague,
and iron twists weapons toward the true north,
and grease refuses to slide in the machinery of progress,
and men feel as free on earth as fleas on the bodies of men,
and lovers no longer whisper to the presence beside them in the dark, *O
corpse-to-be* . . .

And yet perhaps this is the reason you cry,
this the nightmare you wake screaming from:
being forever
in the pre-trembling of a house that falls.

7

Back you go, into your crib.

The last blackbird lights up his gold wings: *farewell.*
Your eyes close inside your head,
in sleep. Already
in your dreams the hours begin to sing.

Little sleep's-head sprouting hair in the moonlight,
when I come back
we will go out together,

we will walk out together among
the ten thousand things,
each scratched too late with such knowledge, *the wages
of dying is love.*

After reading the selection from the poem, pass out copies of it to the students and talk about some of their favorite lines. Tell them that they may not know what all of the lines mean, but they can still use them in their poem and change the meaning if they want to. The assignment is to choose a line that pops out for them and use it as an epigraph the way you showed them on the board or use it as a title of their poem. In either case, they need to be sure to put the line in quotations and then credit Galway Kinnell.

When they read their poems, hold up some of them and point out the use of stanzas and varied line lengths, as well as the quote or epigraph. Here are two student poems.

"Grease Refuses to Slide in the Machinery of Progress" —Galway Kinnell
by Bill, fourth grade

One day the sun
went roller skating
down the side of the world.
Grease would not slide,
doors were closed forever.
The star of darkness
turned to blood.

Finally the sun came out.
Grease slid,
people fell out of their doors
and into mud puddles.
Guns fired at cars.

Then the sun went to its home
in the clouds
and shut the door.
The moon came out
and grease slid
right out of everything
and back into the ground
where it belonged.
But men took it out of trees.

"The Wages of Dying Is Love" —Galway Kinnell
   by Heather, fourth grade

A rose sprouts to show our love.
A bird sings to show our affection.
The sun shines to show our trust.
But on this day a part comes
between us.
We are on different sides of the ocean
except that you are never to be seen again
because the wages of dying
is love.
Darkness comes upon me
as if to tell you will never come back.
As I stand there crying
the wind blows in my face to say to me
love is a cold wind that blows away from you.
Flowers shut up in their lives.
The world stops and I am falling
in a hole
remembering what happened.
I would have invited you
to my lighthouse
to shine the lights
on the troubled sea.
A light flashes in front
of me to take a picture.
But it's really lightning.
The thought of you touches my heart.
I hope you can hear up in heaven.

Chapter Two

Magic Poetry Pencils and Mistake Stickers—"Special Needs Students"

> *I remember the shadow.*
> —Joey, first grade, special education

"Trees Green around the Shed," by Shelley Savren

Six-year-old Lynda sits
cross-legged in the poetry circle.
She won't talk, the teacher confides,
elective mute.

She's a listener.
Stories and poems speak
in her head and jumble on the page.

My hideout I love.
Trees green around the shed.
My friend.

The aide is quick
with her red felt pen fixing words.

In the poetry circle
now it's Lynda's turn to read.
The class chants:
Read your poem, please.

She hesitates, then straightens,
bowing her head into the page
as whispers emerge from her throat
and push the words.

I love my hideout.
It is my friend.
It is at my shed.

Today, many kids with special needs are mainstreamed into regular classrooms with an aide assigned to them; however, sometimes, because of the special need, it's necessary to place students into special education classrooms. Problems arise when these students are seen as "different." But every kid is "different," is "special," and can write poetry. So first, get rid of the label. It's important to give each student what she or he needs, which usually comes down to "attention."

Teaching poetry writing to students with special needs can include all ages and grade levels, from kindergarten through college, some with very unique situations, ranging from being deaf or blind or physically disabled to being developmentally disabled, including autistic or slow learners, for example.

Many of the students who are placed in special-education classrooms or who have any kind of learning disability also have low self-esteem. They often act out when they can't understand what the teacher is teaching and are embarrassed about it. Some might be average learners but live with difficult or abusive situations at home, or their needs are not being met at home and then they act out in school. Alicia, a second-grader, wrote a poem titled "Alone in My House":

> I worry that
> I'm going to die
> because people are shooting a gun
> in my neighborhood
> looking for somebody.

In regular classrooms, sometimes a teacher, who may have tried a variety of solutions but has not been able to stop the disruption, moves the student's seat into the corner or to the end of a row or the front of the classroom, where the teacher can give that student the attention he or she needs and where the student can disturb fewer students.

Sometimes the student feels like he or she is being labeled "bad" but would rather be seen as a "troublemaker" than a "dummy" any day. But guess what? This student loves poetry because he or she gets kudos from the teacher and from the visiting poet for writing anything.

A lot of these students in the corner don't think they can write, when in fact, they can. The teacher or the visiting poet squats at their sides and writes what they say verbatim, skipping spaces, so they can copy the words right under what they dictated. It's amazing what students have inside of them when they don't feel inhibited by their writing skills. They still have vivid imaginations, hurt feelings, and important experiences to share. And sooner or later they write without help.

Before you know it, these students have copied all of the words that were written for them, have earned their stickers, and are proudly drawing a picture. Now they love poetry. It's an old story. Furthermore, it's not unusual for students to transfer their love of poetry to their love of themselves. After the poetry workshop ended in one special education classroom, Shannon, a third-grader, wrote: "I learned to like myself."

With younger students, it's important to bring in the same magic as with regular classrooms. One particular thing that always works well is to use "magic poetry pencils," which are just thicker pencils that have no erasers. Students who have low self-esteem will erase their lives away if given the chance. They write three lines, the visiting poet or teacher acknowledges that they are great lines, moves along, and returns to find the lines erased—gone forever.

These students can be told that poets almost never erase. If they don't like something, they just cross it out with one line because what if they erase it and want it back? They can't get it back. This works. No one can erase.

But some students can't live with crossed-out lines. They say they've made mistakes and have to fix them. So then, the visiting poet or teacher can pull out "mistake stickers" (usually worms or frogs) and put one on the "tragic" mistake. Students learn that something beautiful can be made out of a mistake.

These are usually the same students who don't want to use inventive spelling. They need to be told not to worry about spelling when they're writing because poets don't worry about spelling with a first draft. It's more important that they remember what they wanted to say. Writing has to flow. The challenge, of course, is deciphering what they've written with inventive spelling later on. Teachers are amazingly great at that. Once again, the goal is to get students to love poetry so much that they *want* to write it and feel proud of what they've written and want to share it.

There was a first-grader named Lynda in a special-education class at Kellogg Elementary School in Chula Vista (San Diego County). It was the early 1980s. Lynda was labeled "elective mute." She wouldn't talk at school. She spoke like any other kid at home, but at school, she was silent.

Because it was a special-education classroom, there were only fourteen students, along with a teacher and an aide. Poetry workshop was every week, and the students loved to write. Several of them mixed up the syntax when they wrote, perhaps because they were dyslexic or second-language learners or maybe because they knew they were free to break up language, toss it into the air, and let it fall onto the page in any unique way they wanted.

Since poetry is not necessarily linear, some of the most creative works students wrote had jumbled syntax. It was important for teachers and aides not to correct that syntax, especially since many of the poems were more interesting with jumbled syntax.

In that classroom, students were encouraged to edit their own work if they wished to do so and to fix the spelling by themselves using their word list;

neither the teacher nor the visiting poets corrected it for them—especially while they were still composing the poem. But if they asked for help, then the teacher or visiting poet certainly offered it.

If the students chose not to revise their poems, that was okay, too. However, if the poem went into an anthology or was displayed on a wall, then the teacher or visiting poet asked the students' permission to fix the spelling for them. The important thing at this level was that they write and feel good about it. It was also important for the teacher not to assign a grade to a poem, not even an A.

The next challenge in that classroom was to get students to read their work aloud. Most of them wanted to share their poems. This was first grade, and they weren't as inhibited about sharing as some of the older kids were. Of course, Lynda was silent.

Each week, the students gathered in a circle on the rug at the front of the room before and after they wrote. Everyone wanted to read—except for Lynda. Lynda had never spoken a word at school, but she had words inside her that could come out, so on the last day of poetry workshop, the challenge was to coax them out of her. The class was silent and each student was asked one by one if he or she wanted to hear Lynda's poem.

One by one everyone nodded. Lynda looked down and started to read her poem, and the voice that came out of her was so soft, hardly anyone could hear her. But no one shouted, "I can't hear." They were probably all amazed that Lynda *had* a voice and that she was reading her poem. Even the teacher sat in silent awe as Lynda slowly delivered her words.

Lynda loved sitting in the poetry circle and sharing the poem that she wrote that day. It was a gift for everyone.

SAMPLE WRITING EXERCISES

Note: These exercises are geared toward primary grades, with the understanding that they can be used at all grade levels with the same or different model poems. The student poems are from both regular and special education classrooms.

1) Rhythm: When I'm Mad

The students sit on a rug at the front of the room, and the workshop begins with the usual introduction to poetry and the poetry position. Now the students are ready to do a warm-up lesson, a group poem. This is the best way for these students to get started and gain confidence to write poems on their own.

When they write the group poem, each student contributes a line. There are several different topics to choose from, but today, ask the students to express their anger or hurt feelings, while creating a rhythm. First read a model poem where the speaker gets mad and takes an imaginary journey.

"Mad," by Naomi Shihab Nye

>I got mad at my mother
>so I flew to the moon.
>I could still see our house
>so little in the distance
>with its pointed roof.
>My mother stood in the front yard
>like a pin dot
>searching for me.
>She looked left and right for me.
>She looked deep and far.
>Then I whistled and she tipped her head.
>It gets cold at night on the moon.
>My mother sent up a silver thread
>for me to slide down on.
>She knows me so well.
>She knows I like silver.

Ask the students: "Do you hear any words repeated?" Of course, it's in the last two lines. Talk about how creating a list also makes a rhythm. Then it's time to write a group poem about why "I'm Mad." Ask them to think about why they get mad sometimes. Each student contributes a line. Write the lines on the board or butcher paper or a document camera to be typed and passed out later.

Here are two student poems that repeat words. One is a group poem, and the other was written during an independent assignment on the same topic.

"I'm Mad Because . . . ," group poem, grades 1–2

my mom spanks me
I get in trouble sometimes
my little brother pulls my hair
I have to clean my room
my mom doesn't let me use my bike
my dad is lazy and makes me get his shoes
my hamster wakes me up early in the morning
my mom teases me all the time
my sister fights with me
my dog ran away

the church says just boys can go to the mountains
my mom wouldn't let me paint
my fish died
somebody pushed me on the sidewalk

"Untitled," by Robin, first grade

When I'm mad
I decorate trees.
When I'm mad I go to my room
and punch my pillow.

2) Imagination: Cloud Meeting

Ask the students to imagine that the clouds in the sky are having a meeting to decide what they are going to do. They can decide to rain or create fog, but if the students use their imaginations, they can discover lots of other things that the clouds might want to do. Next read a model poem.

"Almanac: It rains it thaws," by Alicia Ostriker

It rains it thaws the action is wild down there
the silvery cold delicious wetness is trickling in
through tunnels and cracks

whatever tastes it begins to grasp and shove
my god I feel it happening through my shoes
a thousand worms threaded from their mucus cradles

already nudge the softening soil
a thousand rootlets uncurl
trembling icebound fingers

Talk about how the rain can be "silvery cold delicious wetness" and how rain brings out worms, as in this poem. Then ask the students to use their imaginations and think about the clouds up in the sky having a meeting. Ask: "What will they decide to do? Rain? Snow? Create fog? Drop polka dots on the ground?" Encourage them to go wild and find unusual things for clouds to do in their poems.

Here are two student poems resulting from the exercise.

"Clouds," by Alejandra, second grade

Cloud meeting.
    The sun
goes in. The clouds
        turn
            into
        elephants.

"Untitled," by Christina, second grade

My clouds are deciding
if they are going to snow a
unicorn. I think that they are
going to make it snow
a heart. I love a heart so much.

3) Feelings: Friends

First talk about the importance of expressing feelings in poems. Then talk about friends. Ask students what they do with their friends, and you'll get all kinds of answers, ranging from playing with them, telling secrets, sharing ice cream, and so on. Some friends leave them and make them sad, and sometimes they fight with friends, but then they can always make up and be friends again.

Several of these students have bottled up anger inside of them, so tell them that they can express it in words, in a poem, which is a much better way than hitting someone or calling someone a name. Then read a model poem.

"Poem," by Langston Hughes

I loved my friend.
He went away from me.
There is nothing more to say.
The poem ends,
Soft as it began—
I loved my friend.

Tell them that today they're going to write a poem about a special friend and describe what that friend is like and what they do together to make that friendship special. Remind them to *show* or *describe* what they feel, rather than simply stating it.

Here are two student poems. The second poem is by a high-school student in a special education classroom, but younger students can relate to it.

"Untitled," by Jenny, first grade

I have a special friend.
Her name is Andy.
She has a rainbow shirt.
She has a brother.

"Fights," by Joel, twelfth grade

First time I was in a fight,
good thing I won, because if I didn't
my mom would hit me first
for acting dumb and then for getting in a fight.

He swung first, hit me in the jaw.
I swung back, hit him in the lip, started
bleeding. He got scared when he saw blood.
So did I. He started swinging fast, but with all
that blood dripping from his face I knew
I had to end it quick. At the end
of the fight

we had more respect from our friends
a fat lip, a bruised eye and a forgiving heart
for that person we just fought with. At least
that's the way I felt. I felt sorry,
sorry for hurting him and me
in a two minute battle. That fight gave me
a new friend. And for the rest of our lives
we will always back each other up.

4) Similes: What I Like About Myself

First talk about similes. Ask: "How would you describe your teeth? They are white—white like the moon or white like snow. They are sharp—sharp like a needle. Or you can think about your mom. She is soft—soft like a pillow. She is kind—kind like a fairy." Give them some more examples: "My pencil is writing as fast as a train," or "My heart is big like a whole world." They're using "as" or "like" to make a comparison. At this point, the students are all jumping in with examples.

Next, talk about what they like about themselves. Tell them that maybe they're a fast runner or have silky hair or maybe they like to ride a bike. Maybe they like to write poetry! Then read the first four lines of a model poem.

from "A Birthday," by Christina Rossetti

My heart is like a singing bird
  Whose nest is in a watered shoot;
My heart is like an apple tree
  Whose boughs are bent with thickest fruit.
My heart is like a rainbow shell.

Talk about how this poem was written a long time ago, so it rhymes. The speaker is so happy and is celebrating herself using similes when she writes, "My heart is *like* a singing bird," "My heart is *like* an apple tree" and "My heart is *like* a rainbow shell."

Now it's time to write poems that celebrate who they are or say why they like themselves. Encourage them to use similes. Here are two student poems resulting from the exercise. The first one uses similes, and the second one directly says what the speaker likes about himself.

"Untitled," by Jordan, first grade

My hair is yellow
as the moon in the sky.
My eyes are like crystals.
My ears are like shells.
My hands are like a starfish.
My brain is for thoughts
in my head.

"Untitled," by Ati, first grade

I like myself
  because
I got a whole
  bunch of hot
    wheels.

Chapter Three

The Craft of Poetry
Gifted, Seminar, and Pullout Programs

> *a loose collection of relatives*
> *slowly leaving middle age behind*
> *the old patriarch tells stories*
> *mundane really but as magical as ancient myth*
>
> *from* "Family Reunion"
—Matt, eleventh-grade GATE student

"My Sister," by Isabelle, fifth grade

Jean Marie
whose affection is always present,
whose hair gets caught in those little hair barrettes,
who is like a fog horn when angry
and makes me suspect
that her lungs are made of mercury.
To a girl
who I never showed proper respect
and who is now always turning
to my brother for guidance,
who I have turned away from all these years,
and who now is doing the same,
but still locks onto me
those big cow eyes,
but in such a way as to look like a little dove.
Who always wants to be like me,
to wear my clothes,
to learn the things I do.

Whose soft little hands are always taking
other people's things,
but are always giving them back.
A girl who I have never shown my feelings to,
but will try.

Teaching poetry writing is especially rewarding when working in GATE (Gifted and Talented Education) and seminar (students who scored above the ninety-ninth percentile) classrooms. Visiting poets can also do pullout programs for students in regular classrooms (often with GATE students) who excel in writing poetry and are excited to continue working on poetry after the series of workshops has ended in their classes. Teachers can also work with these students right in their classrooms.

When working with these populations, some of the poems that gifted students write are extraordinary, but many are no more amazing than those written by any other students. Imagination and inspiration can be felt by anyone, and every student is "gifted" in some way.

In regular classrooms, GATE and seminar students often have difficulty with the one-size-fits-all curriculums and act bored. Sometimes they want to be challenged. Teachers often find unique ways to expand learning, giving students extracurricular activities; however, truly gifted students will find creative ways to meet challenges on their own. They know how to make subjects interesting.

Some students in the poetry-writing workshops are gifted in some areas, but not in others, and actually feel pressured by all the work that is expected of them. So it becomes important to make poetry a fun activity, not a pressured one.

First do a series of regular workshops in order to generate some poems that students can then revise. Tell the students there are two parts to being a poet: part one is writing poems from inspiration, imagination, and experience, and part two is working on crafting the poem into a piece of art. This is what serious poets do. It seems like hard work, but it's actually a lot of fun. And in the end, they come up with a great product that they can be proud of.

When poems are personal in any way (and some are gut-wrenching), students can easily get their feelings hurt, especially if they have difficulty separating themselves from their poems. Or sometimes they become unwilling to change anything in the poem. Revision, then, becomes a delicate business. It's important to set up ground rules so that everyone feels safe, and no one feels threatened by what others have to say about his or her poems.

Basically, everyone has to respect each author's work, make positive comments about the strengths of the poem, and make suggestions for improvement. Ask the students to address the author directly and ask the author to listen to and consider the critiques. However, ultimately, it is the author's choice to revise or not revise anything in the poem. The poet Denise Levertov said that when every part of a poem is working together, then the poem is finished. That should be the students' yardstick.

Here are guidelines they used for self-critiquing:

Questions That the Author Can Ask Her or Himself When Revising

1. Clarity
   a. Is my meaning clear?
   b. Do I need to tell more—more details? Does my poem come alive through the use of five senses and color?
   c. Do I show—not tell—feelings?
2. Clean up
   a. Are there any wasted phrases or words? Do I repeat unnecessarily?
   b. Word choice: Are my words powerful and precise? Do I use action verbs and strong nouns?
   c. Are my images fresh, new, and concrete—not abstract?
3. Rhythm and form
   a. Does my rhythm flow when I read the poem aloud?
   b. Is my form working to help the poem? Have I checked line breaks and stanzas? Have I tried different options?

When elementary-school GATE students are critiquing their poems as a class or in small groups, they can use the same guidelines outlined in chapter 1, beginning with the student reading the poem aloud and ending with the class scanning it for natural breath lines.

Once the students revise their poems, they can do poetry projects, which include classroom anthologies. One idea is to choose a line from a poem for a title. Some of the titles used in the past are amazing, such as:

- "Today Is the Day to Go Out by Myself"
- "Without You, Aimee, I Would Have Never Made It Through Third Grade"
- "Walking Heart"
- "I Will Play My Worries into a Flute"
- "Snow, the Crisp Sound Pounding"
- "I Took a Bite Through the Rainbow"
- "The Frying Pan with Seven Stars"
- "I Smell Like the Breath of Morning"
- "Fireflies Bring Me Bright Dreams"
- "I Ate the Moon for Breakfast"
- "Fog Up to the Neck of the Beast"

- "Pencil Heaven"
- "To Roam Where the Earth Has Never Traveled."

Another project is making poetry posters. In one GATE pullout program, for grades 1 and 2, students made poetry mobiles with pipe cleaners and pieces of paper with poems written on them. The poems were illustrated on the back and the mobiles were hung from ceilings.

A culminating event at elementary schools is having students read their poems at an assembly, with both GATE and regular classrooms present. Usually parents are invited. At one school, some GATE and seminar students, who were both good poets *and* oral readers, were invited to read on local radio programs. Others read their poems at community locations, such as coffee houses. On one occasion, students came to a gallery with their families, where they were served dinner and then read their poems. Needless to say, on all of these occasions, parents and grandparents were very proud.

At Sunset View Elementary School in San Diego, there were three extremely gifted students who were siblings and who had poetry-writing workshops in their classes for two years. The youngest, Jean, was in first and second grade, and at the end of the second year, she had just been certified for GATE. Her older sister Isabelle was a GATE student in fourth and fifth grade, and she was just about to enter the seminar program in sixth grade. Their brother Mike had been in the seminar class for both fifth and sixth grades.

At the end of the second year, a local TV station wanted three students to be interviewed, along with the visiting poet, and to read their poems. Jean, Isabelle, and Mike went. They interviewed like pros and were proud to read their poems and have them broadcasted on TV. Their poems—and they each wrote many—were all gems. This chapter begins with a poem by Isabelle, and Mike's poem "Juniper" is used as a sample for the first exercise. Here is a poem by Jean:

"The Scissor Clouds," by Jean, first grade

I am the clouds
cutting my way through the moon.
The people are
               f
            a
           l
          l
         i
        n
       g
in the water.

I see a girl
standing on the bridge.
Her eyes are as round as the moon.
But how can that be?
It's me.

SAMPLE WRITING EXERCISES

NOTE: This chapter just presents the writing prompt and resulting poems by students. There are no model poems by professional poets. Although the focus of this chapter is primarily on elementary-school students, the poems presented here are also by middle-school GATE students and high-school Honors and Advanced Placement students.

1) Imagination/Imagery: Going Out in Nature

Ask students to think about a time when they were in nature, either camping, hiking, swimming, fishing—doing any activity outdoors. Ask them to remember what they can and then to use their imaginations to fill in other details, as long as they are true to the emotion behind the poem. Encourage them to use fresh, sensual imagery that will make the poem come alive.

"Juniper," by Mike, fifth grade

The night blooming juniper reaches out,
but hesitates
for that is its nature.
Collapses itself
forever like a trap door
one way
for that is its custom.
Condensed from the world,
shyness controls its actions
except in twilight
when it unfolds like a Monarch,
damp and shivering
upon a violet haze.

"Untitled," by Mikey, fifth grade

I remember the fall leaves falling
and the cool breeze of Blackport
New York Lake.
Even though my father died
I can have a nice time.

The horizon on the lake,
it has the strike of light.

"A Leaf that Meets the Eye," by Danielle, fourth grade

A leaf, how green,
its veins rushing through the blood
of a Northern star
equipped with early afternoon dew,
just waiting for a better and more graceful tomorrow.
It waits for the scent
of an ugly mortal's rotten breath
to crush it with a moldy Reebok shoe.
It waits for an eerie (but young) skunk
to lay its smelly tail
upon its now crumbling stem.
But now, it is no longer green.
It is tattered, crumbled, a wisp-o-the-willows,
an old ugly pile of dust,
lying hot in the midday sun.
Its gentle world is gone.
Now, so elderly, strict and long.
Its veins of starlight
have blindly whisked away.
Too late, all gone now,
says the two-year-old's sense of care
to its wooden forest of lonely places,
stricken clear upon the gale.

2) Feelings: Friends and Relatives

Ask the students to write a portrait poem describing someone around their age—someone they play with or spend time with; someone they trust and care about. Tell them to talk about that person, describing what he or she is like and what they do together. It's important to let their feelings toward that person come through in the description without stating them.

"My Brother," by Cameron, sixth grade

You are there.
You are always there like a tick
that burrows into hot flesh.
You follow me out in the day
and play Nintendo with me
when it is night.
We laugh together at sitcoms
and blare the radio as we do our homework.

Sometimes I scream at you
to get out of my room.
But when I am alone
I miss your company.
So when you peek around the door
I let you stay.

"Untitled," by Allison, fifth grade

She has strawberry hair
    blue-gray eyes.
She's wearing on off-white
top with stripes of rainbow
    colors.
When she writes she
kind of lays her head on the
desk, she's my friend.
    She writes slowly
        and carefully.
    She erases
    the word
    and uses another
    one.
        She doesn't
    talk just
        sighs.

"My Cousin," by Jonathan, sixth grade

I don't remember much about him,
but I mostly remember
the summer of '91,
both of us running through
the cold wet leaves barefoot.
Running around right outside
our family's cabin in Massachusetts
after a summer rainstorm.
I remember taking our short boat rides
on Lake Mascuppic and exploring
Patmos Island, looking for treasure.
I remember New Years Eve in Florida
of '87 . . . . I remember the phone call
from my grandparents who
lived in Florida . . . . It didn't have
to happen to Collen. He was
only 13, but that's life, I guess.

He died in 1992, hung himself.
Collen was a dear friend. We
all loved him. I still remember
the summers with Collen.

3) Personification: Concept Poems

First, make a list on the board of "concept" words, nouns that are not persons, places, things or animals, but abstract things that cannot be touched. The list includes: anger, sorrow, jealousy, loneliness, fear, apathy, grief, hunger, death, bitterness, happiness, love, hatred, pride, and so on.

Then ask students to personify each concept—give it a life. For example, jealousy could brush its teeth and put on lipstick, wanting to look its best for all the boys; loneliness could live in a closet listening to cracking sounds in the floor; and happiness could go dancing on the moon. Also encourage the students to use metaphors and similes to describe their concepts.

"Drowning in Him," by Becky, ninth grade

Depression drowns me.
I can feel his hands pushing me further down
    in the water.
I struggle to get out of his grasp.
I try everything: pills, cuts and bruises.
I'm powerless against him.
He takes over me.
He speaks to me in the silky night
    telling me I'm wrong, that nobody cares.
He controls my mind, making me
    think of only dark morbid thoughts.
He pushes me to the end with his
    big, heavy hands.
I don't know what to do.
The only way I know how to get out
    is by killing myself, but he doesn't let me.
Now when I'm sad, I look for comfort
in Depression . . . . He has me under his control.

"Apathy," by Laura, ninth grade

He shows up at my front door,
Wearing nothing
Because he doesn't care.

I invite him in.
He tracks mud all over

My mother's Persian rug
But doesn't stop to say,
"I'm sorry."

He sits down and puts his feet
On the glass coffee table
And picks his nose,
An wipes it on the couch,
Not caring how grotesque he is.

He turns on the T.V.
And puts it on the Home Shopping Network
Like he's really watching it anyway.

He takes my cool glass of lemonade
And chugs it so that it
Drips down his glossy cheeks.
"So? he says.

He leaves my home.
The door shuts behind him,
As he waltzes down the street
Not having a care in the world.

He is . . . my apathy.

"Death," by Josephine, seventh grade

He stands at the top of his kingdom
and he owns the blue ripples
at the pit of the land
and the fading fire in the sky.
The green treasure in his pocket
is nothing to him.
If he were to let one or the other
dance far away into the wind,
the green treasure
he would let fly
like elegant swans.
Black eyes stare into the mountain.
His eyes so old,
his skin pale and wrinkled
but soft.
A silk shirt and a tailored suit
protect him from death's breeze.
and a tear drops from his black eyes
to add to the ripples of violet water.
For he is waiting for darkness.

At once he falls.
His garments no longer protect him.
And innocent eyes let him sleep
in death's lonely breeze.

4) Details: Portraits and Motion Picture Poems

Ask the students to make family portraits of a parent or grandparent using lots of details, describing that person's behavior, revealing secrets, really giving the reader an inside view into that person's life. An artist should be able to paint the portrait of what he or she described in words. Ask them to create motion pictures, so that a filmmaker could make a film from what they describe in the poem. Tell them not to hold back, but to allow all of their feelings about that person to come through in the images they create.

"Soap Opera," by Chris, eleventh grade

this is too surreal
it's the stuff soap operas are made of
the shows mom used to watch sometimes
but not anymore . . .
now that the stories are about us
now that dad has become the man
who takes his coat and hat and leaves every night
not coming back until morning . . .
now that mom has become the woman
who waits at home sitting on the bed
crying . . .
now that I have become the child
confused with the new load of worries
who is now sullen . . . withdrawn
it feels like someone should be watching us
crying at the sad parts
when the man ignores the woman's pleas and walks out the door
getting angry at the controversy
when the child confronts his father
wondering what will happen next . . .
hoping as I do to avoid the agonizing feeling
of an episode that ends with:
to be continued . . .

"Cowboy Bill," by Evelyn, eleventh grade

I stroll through the corral,
trying to tolerate the smell
of fresh manure.

You ride up on your chocolate-dust horse.
I can almost taste the cigarette hanging
out the side of your chapped lips,
just by the smell.

I wonder if you like me.
I wonder if you notice how I stick out
like a sore thumb,
a city girl in your country world.

A cloud of smoke hangs about your
hat-topped head.
And the rolling green hills of Santa Paula
1919 spread out behind you,
as if they are streaming from
the back of your mind,
the setting of your memories.

I wonder how it could possibly be
that you are my grandfather,
a tough cowboy, a Marlboro man
with a red flannel and boots
and me a tender-footed stranger
who lives in a foreign world
and doesn't recognize you.

"Father," by Cameron, eleventh grade

Ducking through the door,
striding across the room,
      he came.
His square face set with a smile,
      His eyes round and dark,
      sparkling by the light.
Five steps and he was across my living room.
      There I was standing,
      a smile on my face.
      There I was standing
looking straight up for miles just to see his face.
His massive hand came down,
      lightly patting me on the head.
Using both hands,
      he effortlessly lifted me into the air.
      From way up there,
I saw my home in a whole new way.
I laughed, I giggled . . . I was happy.

He said he couldn't stay long,
    but that was all right.
I knew he would be back,
    and that's all that mattered.
He placed me on the floor
    and said good-bye.
I watched him vanish that night,
    eight years to this day.

Chapter Four

Poetry Outside the Classroom

*The spring leaves
are waving
pretty on the rocks.*

—Jennifer, kindergarten

"The Star," by Shelley Savren

Young, golden-haired and on one knee,
I bend to pour two jugs of water
into a royal rippling pond,
feeding nighttime secrets to the day,
changing rich and wild words to melody.

But when the sun dips down
I'll rise and be a swirling silver bell.
I'll hide inside the clouds
when they rollout thunder blasts
and lightning with its bridge of zaps.

Look for me on warm clear nights
shining like a firefly.
All the kids will leap to catch me,
as they dance and gleam
in a summer forest on a patch of green.

Poetry writing can be taught almost anywhere—at libraries, community centers, after-school programs, homeschool programs, and more. Students who come to poetry workshops outside of classrooms are usually excited to write poetry, or sometimes their parents sign them up and often pay for the programs. In either case, they don't have to be convinced that writing poetry is great. Still, it is important to not make the workshops seem too academic. Participants should feel that this is a special program and is different from school.

You can use a lot of the same exercises that are used in the classroom and have great results. And because the students are not in school, they are usually more relaxed. Students can move around the room freely, but they need to focus on what we're doing. It is fun for them to do a lot of art projects that go with poetry, like making cards with poems or poetry posters and even poetry books.

Except for when the workshops take place in libraries, the students can go outside to write, weather permitting. You can make up poetry word games with them and take advantage of the settings they're in, using their five senses to experience their surroundings. All of that can be brought into their poems.

Some of the students who participated in these programs over the years truly became committed writers, and some were just along for the good time. Even though the focus was on the process of poetry writing, the students always went home with a finished project, which included a poem. The best part about *these* workshops was that the students all had fun. And if students are having fun writing poems, they'll want to keep writing them.

SAMPLE WRITING EXERCISES

1) Five Senses: Listening to the World Outside

Talk about how people don't always pay attention to their five senses and why it's important to use them in poetry in order to make their poems come alive. Then read an excerpt from a model poem.

from "Song of Myself," section 26, by Walt Whitman

Now I will do nothing but listen,
To accrue what I hear into this song, to let sounds contribute toward it.

I hear bravuras of birds, bustle of growing wheat, gossip of flames, clack of sticks
    cooking my meals,
I hear the sound I love, the sound of the human voice,
I hear all sounds running together, combined, fused or following,

Sounds of the city, and sounds out of the city, sounds of the day and night,
Talkative young ones to those that like them, the loud laugh of work-people at
    their meals,
The angry base of disjointed friendship, the faint tones of the sick,
The judge with hands tight to the desk, his pallid lips pronouncing a death-
    sentence,

The heave'e'yo of stevedores unlading ships by the wharves, the refrain of the
    anchor-lifters,
The ring of alarm-bells, the cry of fire, the whirr of swift-streaking engines and
    hose-carts with premonitory tinkles, and color'd lights,
The steam-whistle, the solid roll of the train of approaching cars,
. . . .

I hear the violoncello ('tis the young man's heart's complaint,)
I hear the key'd cornet, glides quickly in through my ears,
It shakes mad-sweet pangs through my belly and breast.

I hear the chorus, it is a grand opera,
Ah, this indeed is music—this suits me.

Talk about all the sounds that Whitman heard outside, like "bustle of growing wheat, gossip of flames, clack of sticks cooking my meals," and "the whirr of swift-streaking engines and hose-carts. . . ." Then take the group outside and have them walk around silently for about five minutes, doing nothing but listening.

When the students come back inside, ask them to sit down silently. Write the words, "Now I will do nothing but listen" on the board and tell the students to copy the words on their paper and on the count of three to begin to write about all the sounds they heard and sounds that they could imagine. Another choice is to write about being outside and experiencing it with at least one or two of their five senses. Or if they want, they can write about being inside, too. Encourage them to also focus on other senses.

Here are two student poems using some of their five senses. The first one takes place outside and the second moves into a grandma's kitchen.

"Untitled," by Michelle, fifth grade

Today
is
the day
to go
out by
myself
crossing
the rocks
exploring
the world
taking my
walks at
the park.

I feel
like I
am floating
down a stream.

"My Grandma," by Paul, sixth grade

My grandma lives just down the street.
I hear cars driving by as my feet
clomp against the sidewalk.
I walk in the back door
and see my reflection
on the shiny newly-waxed floor.
I see my grandmother
pulling some hot Yorkshire
Pudding out of the oven.
It's so tempting my mouth is watering.
I reach to get some, but she tips
my hand with her big wooden spoon.
She says it's for dinner.
I tell her dinner is in ten whole minutes.

I can't wait any longer.
I am gasping for it.
My grandma starts dinner early
and I run to my seat
first dibs on the pudding.
I snatch the biggest piece
and pour the gravy on thick.
My grandma looks at me and smiles.

2) Color: Creating Something Colorful

Talk about the importance of using color in poems. Students can create a poem where color is not only present, but is important. Then read a model poem.

"The Red Wheelbarrow," by William Carlos Williams

so much depends
upon

a red wheel
barrow

glazed with rain
water

beside the white
chickens.

This seems like a simple poem, but the colors are important in order to paint a picture of the scene. Ask the students to write a poem that begins with an ordinary or unusual color. Or they can use the color as a title. The poem can either describe the color using their imaginations or use it as an adjective to describe something else. For example, brown can be mud on a mountain or can be brown hiking boots that climb a mountain.

Here are two student poems.

"Silver," by Adam, fourth grade

Silver is like thousands of glittery lakes,
like lots of waterfalls,
silvery mongooses,
silvery dragons.
Like tinfoil in the sun,
all glittery, like dew on leaves.

"The Thistle Dragon," by Paul, fourth grade

The thistle dragon stands in the front
of the Chinese parade.
Tall, clear, it starts to dance.
Its head shakes
as people in the stands cheer.
The tail sways.
The thistle dragon dances
in the golden sunset.

3) Imagery and Persona: Using Picture Cards

Talk about imagery and the meaning of the word "persona," writing in first person from someone else's point of view. Then pass out picture cards. Tarot cards are great for this exercise because they have wonderful, detailed pictures. Read a short part of a model poem based on a tarot card.

from "The Total Influence or Outcome of the Matter: THE SUN," by Marge Piercy

The sun is rising, feel it: the air smells fresh.
I cannot look in the sun's face, its brightness blinds me,
but from my own shadow becoming distinct
I know that now at last
it is beginning to grow light.

Next, give each student a picture card or a tarot card and ask the students to imagine that they are the person in that picture and to write from that point of view, in a persona. Encourage them to make up a life for the person, based on what they see and feel, using strong images to describe the person and his or her surroundings.

Here are two student poems each written from tarot cards.

"The Fool," by Olivia, fifth grade

The sun shines in my face
as I try
to see
the snowy mountains.

I am a fool.

I have the power
of the sun.

My white snow dog
follows me
through the pasture.

I throw my white lucky flower
into the sea below me.

I sleep on the edge
of the sky.

I pack leaves, shells and magic
in my bag that I carry.

My hair is as green as a grape
and I have the power of the wind.

"The 8 of Swords," by Melissa, fifth grade

I am inside a world that does not exist.
Don't ask me why I'm here.
The shadow upon darkness
is coming up my backbone.
I fear but don't know what.
I am very lonely.
I can't talk to myself
because I don't know where I am.
I don't know where I am
because there's nowhere to be.

4) Details: Odes

First, talk about the importance of using details in poems. Then talk about the concept of odes. It's a tribute honoring someone. Traditionally, odes were written to "my fair lady" or to queens and people of high honor. But contemporary odes can be honoring anyone or anything, even something silly. Read a model poem.

"Ode to Pablo's Tennis Shoes," by Gary Soto

They wait under Pablo's bed,
Rain-beaten, sun-beaten,
A scuff of green
At their tips
From when he fell
In the school yard.
He fell leaping for a football
That sailed his way.
But Pablo fell and got up,
Green on his shoes,
With the football
Out of reach.

Now it's night.
Pablo is in bed listening
To his mother laughing
to the Mexican *novelas* on TV.
His shoes, twin pets
That snuggle his toes,
Are under the bed.
He should have bathed,
But he didn't.
(Dirt rolls from his palm,
Blades of grass
Tumble from his hair.)
He wants to be
Like his shoes,
A little dirty
From the road,
A little worn
From racing to the drinking fountain
A hundred times in one day.
It takes water
To make him go,
And his shoes to get him
There. He loves his shoes,
Cloth like a sail,
Rubber like
A lifeboat on rough sea.
Pablo is tired,
Sinking into the mattress.
His eyes sting from

Grass and long words in books.
He needs eight hours
Of sleep
To cool his shoes,
The tongues hanging
Out, exhausted.

Talk about how this poem is about Pablo, but mainly honors his tennis shoes, which have a life of their own, complete with tongues. Now it's time for students to write a poem that is an ode or a tribute, a poem honoring something or someone. It can be an object, like a tomato or tennis shoes, or it can be a person they admire and want to pay tribute to. Remind them to use lots of details in their poems.

Here are two student ode poems.

"Ode to Aimee Wood," by Jami, sixth grade

Without you, Aimee, I
would have never made
it through third grade.
You're like pudding. You're
my best friend.
We have had the best laughs looking
at things and people. And
I would never have broken
my nails.

"Ode to my Hair," by Tammy, fifth grade

Hair, you always
stick out, you drive
      me crazy.
Sometimes you
      look
beautiful like
    a
unicorn floating
      through
the air. But
sometimes you
look like
a mighty warrior. And
      sometimes you
           are as
greasy as an onion. I
just don't understand you.

Chapter Five

Poetry in the Face of Art
Writing in an Art Museum

"Girl with the Red Flower"

Sad, mad, lonely
red, purple
in the house.
She was painting
an empty heart.

—Bryan, kindergarten

"Shepherd Girl," by Shelley Savren
after William Bouguereau's *The Young Shepherdess*

Sheep graze the chartreuse meadow
in an endless rolling landscape
and the shepherd girl turns away
confident in their contentment. Her gaze
is a brilliant invitation to a convention of clouds
gathering up afternoon sky.

She is looking at someone, holding back
expression, hiding branches in her hands
behind her back. A pinstriped apron
falls gently over blue gathers
of skirt and the orange-lined strap
has journeyed down her shoulder, loosening
a white, cuffed-sleeve, peasant blouse.

Silence cloaks cherry-tight lips,
her neck curves, soft brown eyes
longing. Her bronze hair is bundled,

but loose strands have gone astray. She knows
the heat of summer, and her clean, bare
feet caress the ground near a pile of pebbles.

She is waiting for someone
to enter this picture, take her up
into the sweet axis of arms
and transport her to another landscape, cool,
like iced cocoa, and not so quiet.

In the early 1990s, the San Diego Museum of Art had a program called Young at Art, and they wanted to have a visiting poet conduct poetry-writing workshops in the galleries on a few Saturdays. The workshops were for parents and their children and were presented in collaboration with the museum's educational staff. It was truly a wonderful program.

Then after having a visiting poet at Sunset View Elementary School in San Diego for six years, students were eager to try combining two genres: visual art and poetry. Every single classroom at Sunset View took one or more field trips to the museum for morning-long workshops. The classes rotated turns on every Wednesday.

Each classroom went into different galleries, including the sculpture garden outside, and a docent talked with the students about the paintings or sculptures there. She addressed the colors and the moods they created and pointed out how the lines formed certain rhythms. And of course, she talked with students about the content and asked them what they thought the artist was trying to communicate.

This kind of field trip can be arranged with any art museum. After the docent speaks about the art, ask the students what they see when they look at each painting *and* how the painting makes them feel. Ask them what they imagine the story behind each painting to be. They learn that paintings are a window into the artist's life.

Then the students discuss each painting in terms of a poetic concept, such as imagery or the five senses or rhythm. Next, read model poems and student poems that you match up with the paintings and ask the students to write poems based on an art piece of their choice and the poetic concept that you have introduced.

Students at Sunset View Elementary School loved the field trips, and some classes went back to visit different galleries over the course of the year. After a large batch of poems was written, about thirty-five students were chosen, a sampling from each class, to revise their poems in a pullout program.

Once the revisions were completed, a visual artist, Tama Dumlau, came on campus and worked with the chosen students to illustrate their poems. In the end, there were the original pieces of art, the ekphrastic poems (poems inspired by art), and the drawings the students created to go with their poems.

Then Tama had each student mount his or her poem and drawing as one piece of art. It was quite a collection.

After the projects were completed, the museum arranged to have an exhibit of the work. They titled it "Poetry in the Face of Art." They chose a corridor in the museum and hung the pieces. They also hosted a great reception for the students and their parents and siblings, along with the press. Each student stood by his or her art piece and read her or his poem. It was an amazing event.

The exhibit hung there for two weeks and was then moved to a local coffeehouse in the school's neighborhood. Needless to say, the entire program was a great accomplishment for everyone. Parents, especially, took pride in their children's work.

SAMPLE WRITING EXERCISES

Note: The pictures for these exercises can be found in the book *San Diego Museum of Art: Selected Works* (ISBN: 0-937108-31-6), which is published by the museum. The pictures can be placed under a document camera for the students to see. If you do not have the book, the pictures can be found on Google Images, or other similar pictures will work, as well.

1) Imagination: Stepping Inside a Painting

Begin by talking about three paintings and what's going on in them. The first painting is "The Young Shepherdess" (1885, oil on canvas), by William Bougereau. It depicts a peasant girl in rural France. She's dressed in traditional shepherdess garb and is barefoot. Her hair is tied in a bun, and she is looking directly at the artist with her brown eyes, smooth skin, and expressionless face. Sheep are in the background. Ask the students, "What is the shepherdess thinking or feeling?"

The next painting is "Man Fording a Stream" (1872, oil on canvas), by Jean-Baptiste Camille Corot. It shows a French landscape of rocks and trees surrounding a creek, with a man walking with his cane. The time is either just before dusk or just after dawn, with clouds in the background and traces of blue sky. The light on the rocks, water, trees, and leaves gives a message of celebrating nature. The man walking with a stick in the stream appears to be on an adventure, enjoying the water and its surroundings. Ask the students, "Where might he be headed?"

The third painting is "The Hands of Dr. Moore" (1940, oil on canvas), by Diego Rivera. It features the hands of a surgeon carving a tree that is shaped like a woman. The tree's lower limbs are wounded and discolored, and the hands, holding a scalpel, are amputating the limb. The wound is red, clearly the color of human blood, not the color of a dead limb. The tree appears to be symbolic of the Tree of Life, carrying lights in its branches. Ask the students, "What can you imagine the tree feels?"

Next, read a model poem that fits with the theme of one of the paintings, in this case, the "Man Fording a Stream." The poet is celebrating the water in the stream.

"Running Water Music II," by Gary Snyder

Clear running stream
              clear running stream

Your water is light
              to my mouth
And a light to my dry body

              your flowing
Music,
              in my ears. free,

Flowing free!
With you
              in me.

Ask the students to write poems based on one of the paintings. Tell them to climb inside the painting and imagine that they are that person or that tree or the hands. Ask them to imagine what they are thinking or feeling and what they are going to do next.

Here are three student poems based on those paintings.

"The Lady," by Marisa, first grade, responding to "The Young Shepherdess"

She looks like me,
shiny black hair
soft brown skin,
eyelashes dabbed with sparkly oil
eyes blossoming with color.

"I Would Go Fishing," by Kevin, kindergarten, responding to "Man Fording a Stream"

If I were at a lake
I would go fishing and swimming
with mommy.
Then we would walk by the river.
The stream sounds
like ice cream dripping off the cone.

**"The Tree of Life," by Joey, fourth grade, responding to
"The Hands of Dr. Moore"**

The tree stands lifeless,
its breath stolen
its heart in eternal sleep.
As it sinks into the ground,
new buds grow on its trembling branches.
Its brilliant trunk gleams like fire
and its limbs stretch
and break through the moist new soil
like quivering snakes.
And there it stands
like a silver statue
in the golden sunlight.

2) Imagery: Forces of Nature and People's Relationship to Nature

First, review the importance of using imagery in poems. Now have the students look at the pictures and create their own pictures with their words. They can use similes and personification in their poems and compare what they see to other things, or they can *become* something in the painting.

Then look at the individual paintings. The first one is titled "Winter Road" (1912, oil on canvas), by George Wesley Bellows. It takes place in New York and shows snow-covered terrain beyond a clear lake behind a house and trees. In the foreground, a man is walking in the snow. The day is clear and bright, and trees cast shadows in the snow, contrasting the brilliant white on this obviously frigid day. Ask the students how the snow affects everything in the painting—the man walking, the trees, the people they can imagine in the house.

The next painting is "Shipwreck" (1834, oil on canvas), by Thomas Doughty. It is of a Boston seascape. A storm is brewing with high waves and dark clouds in the background. On one side is a tree on a cliff, and on the other are trees on an embankment. All the trees are being fiercely blown by the wind. There is a tiny image of a man on a rock looking out into the ocean at a ship breaking up. Discuss what it would feel like to be on that ship or watching it. Ask the students, "What do the waves look like, sound like?"

The third painting is "Eve of Saint John" (1960, tempura on board), by Peter Hurd. It is a Southwest prairie painting, with a wide landscape and a cowboy on a horse and a lit farmhouse in the background. It is dusk. In the foreground, a young girl with long, brown hair, wearing jeans and a sleeveless, white shirt holds a candle in one hand—which illuminates her face. Her other hand is protecting the flame from going out. Although she is standing still in the painting, the assumption is that she is on her way somewhere;

perhaps, as hinted in the title, to church. Ask the students, "Where do you think she is headed at night?" "Where is the cowboy in the distance going that evening?" "What images do each of these paintings present?"

Then read a model poem about snow, relating it to "Winter Road."

"Dream of Snow," by Glenna Luschei

The winds hum through icicles.
This is where the thistles blow,
this is where the souls go
to listen to the flute.

I will rattle the pods.

I cannot see through the milkweed.
I cannot reach the blizzard.
Why am I here?
Have I come to sing for my father?

Hold
the opal of my heart
until it warms.

Now it's time to write poems with images, pictures made out of words, and consider the force of nature. The world is controlled by what's happening outside: snow, wind, and storms or oncoming darkness. Ask the students to think about how people in the paintings relate to that and to consider, "What is a winter day like?" "What might it be like to be on a ship in the water during a storm?" "What is it like to walk alone in the dark with just a candle?" Tell them that they can enter the pictures and become something in it, using personification, or they can describe what they see and use similes, if they'd like.

Here are three student poems inspired by those paintings.

"Untitled," by Aaron, third grade, responding to "Winter Road"

Snow on windswept peaks
with cloud surroundings.
A slight whistle of the wind zooming past trees
like a cheetah with its tail on fire.
The trees asleep or winter, covered with snow
like a thick winter blanket
with freezing water
and with a monstrous chill.

"The Stormy Day," by Rachel, first grade, responding to "Shipwreck"

I am the huge waves
hitting the rocks!

I am a red crab
weaving in and out of
shells.
I am a great white shark
Scrambling!

"Flame," by Alyson, sixth grade, responding to "Eve of Saint John"

I am a flame
flickering in the wind.
I am hot, but yielding.
I do not scorch or burn.
I am a golden teardrop
that cannot melt,
a shining flare for the world,
a guide, untormented by the dark.
I make light
for my carrier to see.
I flutter on a candle
and roar on a fire.
I stand in the hollow of your heart
and drive away fear
created by blackness.
I am a flame,
flickering in the wind.

3) Color: Miracle of Blossoming and Color as an Expression of Mood

Review the importance of color in poems. In paintings, colors can create a mood. If the painting has dark colors, viewers might feel sad. Bright colors might make people happy and pastels might make them feel calm. Ask students how different colors make them feel.

Then look at what colors people are wearing and look at the colors in the paintings. The first painting is "Narcissi and Hyacinths" (1950, watercolor), by Emil Nolde. It shows a bright bouquet of flowers in a natural setting, not in a vase. Bright blue, yellow, and red top the bright green stems on a golden background. The mood in this watercolor is lively, one of hope and optimism, given the time period after World War II in Germany.

The next painting is "The White Flower" (1932, oil on canvas), by Georgia O'Keeffe. It is an oil painting of a trumpet flower. The viewer is looking directly into the enlarged flower, and the white is emphasized by shadows and a blue reflection behind it. The flower looks soft, and the viewer feels like she or he can easily climb inside and slide down its petals. Ask the students how it would feel to be inside the white flower.

The third painting is "Red Blossom" (1910, oil on board), by Alexej von Jawlensky. It depicts a girl, perhaps of wealth or royalty, in a bright blue dress with a yellow collar. She is holding a bright red blossom that looks like a heart near her real heart. The face of the girl is somewhat abstract, with black lines for her features and thick black lines for her hair. Her mouth is just a straight line, presenting a solemn or sad mood. Ask the students why the girl might not look happy.

Next, read a model poem about a red flower, which you can relate to the painting "Red Blossom."

"Three Worlds," by Sam Hamill

From the split, dry trunk
of a three-hundred-year-old
tsubaki tree, one
fragile new twig with three leaves
holds a perfect red flower.

Now it's time to write poems with lots of colors in them. The students can write about the flower or blossom that the person in the painting is holding, they can write about how the colors make them feel, or they can write about blossoming—the life cycle of a flower, real or imaginary.

Here are three student poems.

"I Am a Fairy Flower," by Joanne, second grade, responding to "Narcissi and Hyacinths"

The flower spirits go into their flowers
and fold up their wings
then take a long winter nap.

When spring comes
they fly out
and dance all about the flowers.
Winter is over,
the flowers bloom
red, white, pink, blue, orange, purple.

I am the fairy flower queen.
It is time to go to sleep.
The fairies help the queen clean up.
Then they fluff up their flowers
so they are soft.

"Two Trumpets," by Crystal, fifth grade, responding to "The White Flower"

A little flower starts to perish,
its roots like a balloon out of breath.
But its petals open light colors

bloom, disappearing
into winter's bitter snow.

When bluebirds chirp again
and start to make their homes
where that little flower once stood,
a new flower will take its place.
White and green petals, yellow tips
will bloom
like a trumpet blowing its horn.

"The Magic Rose," by Alina, second grade, responding to "Red Blossom"

A fairy is locked up in a blossom
and down
        down comes a fan.
She doesn't know where it came from.
Her arms wave the purple turquoise fan
and she flies out.
The red blossom.

4) Feelings: Comings and Goings

Review the importance of expressing feelings in poems. Then talk about how sometimes when people leave, there is a loss in their hearts and they feel sad. Yet sometimes leaving is a good thing. People leave to go on vacations, for example. And then they return. But sometimes people leave and don't return.

Then discuss the two paintings and the sculpture. The first piece is "Aluminum Horse #5" (1982, steel and fused aluminum), by Deborah Butterfield. It is a wire sculpture of a horse, head bent, with stilts for legs. There is no mane or features, but based on the posing of the horse, the animal looks unhappy. It could be searching for something, perhaps food. Ask the students to imagine where the horse has been and where it is going.

The next piece is "Moon Landscape" (1925, oil on canvas), by Max Beckmann. It is a scene in Germany of a river flowing around a bend, with two pieces of land on either side. In the foreground the landscape has houses and rows of trees. In the background, the landscape is of buildings.

Tones of green echo throughout the painting; for example, there is a green cast over the white water. The green skyline consists of two long lines of gray clouds with a white full moon behind it. In the immediate foreground, four pedestrians are looking at the water from a bridge. One figure is alone on the left, and three people huddle together. Ask the students what the people on the bridge are looking at. "Are they watching someone who just left or waiting for someone to arrive or just looking at the moon?"

The third piece is "The Seine in Paris" (ca. 1940, oil on canvas), by Raoul Dufy. It has an impressionistic flavor of blended pastels. The scene is along the Seine, with two boats docked and one small boat making waves. It appears to be leaving down the waterway. Above is a landscape of trees and building tops. In the foreground is an orange, white, and blue flag waving in the wind, similar to the flag of France (which has thick red, white, and blue stripes). The orange color provides contrast to the blues in the painting. Ask the students to imagine someone leaving or arriving on one of the boats.

Then read a model poem about a moon rising over water, which corresponds with the painting "Moon Landscape."

"The Moon Rising," by Federico Garcia Lorca, translated by Lysander Kemp

When the moon rises,
the bells hang silent,
and impenetrable footpaths
appear.

When the moon rises,
the sea covers the land,
and the heart feels
like an island in infinity.

Nobody eats oranges
under the full moon.
One must eat fruit
that is green and cold.

When the moon rises,
moon of a hundred equal faces,
the silver coinage
sobs in the pocket.

Now it's time to write. Talk again about the idea of comings and goings and how they feel when people leave and when they arrive, about how a moonrise can make them feel and about what they can imagine the life of a metal horse to be like. It could be a happy life or a sad life, depending on what happens.

Then tell the students to use their imaginations and get inside the art piece and make up a story behind it. It can be a story about coming or going or loss or anything they want. They can be in the poem, or they can write about what's going on in the art piece. But their feelings should come through in the poem without their stating them.

Here are three student poems based on the paintings.

"The Shooting Field," by Jajie, third grade, responding to "Aluminum Horse #5"

In the warm breeze
where flowers sway and horses run
the men shoot.
I cover my eyes with my hands,
my gentle hands.
There is blood everywhere
and when I go to sleep
I dream of it
all night long.

"Night Landscape," by Sarah, sixth grade, responding to "Moon Landscape"

I look out upon the silvery grey water
where a giant glittering far-away star
has fallen into the depths of the silent river.
Its calmness fills my body,
cooling my scarlet blood.

The strangers around me on the bridge
suddenly feel like old friends.
We huddle together for warmth
on the bleak winter night
and share our secrets
while staring into the starless, feelingless sky.

Two barren clouds
call out for companionship,
pleading for us to come up
and play moon tag.
But they cut the moon
and we can't catch it.
One streetlight burns a dull orange
about the silvery grey water,
warming my scarlet blood
as the night stands still.

"La Seine á Paris," by Linda, fourth grade, responding to "The Seine in Paris"

On a sunny Paris morning
she left without saying goodbye.
It touched my heart
like a rainy day in winter.
She left on a boat
where the sea smells like fresh gardenias,
where we once swam
and shared our secrets.
She left me
with no doors
no maps
no path to follow
no bridges
no future
in Paris in the middle of nowhere.
I just can't believe she left.

Chapter Six

Home Is Where You Sleep at Night
Homeless, Abused, and Neglected Students

> *My mom always yells at me
> for everything. Even if I did not do it she yells
> at me still, because she does not love me, only
> my sisters. I am the young one in the family. My
> dad is mean. I hate him.*
>
> —Tina, third grade

"The Court School," by Shelley Savren

Her face was a welt
and her brown hair chopped to a crew.
Jumped by a gang of girls, was all she said.
This was her chance to write anything
she wanted, but she shouted,
Go ___ yourself and your poetry, too.

It was different the next week.
She was quiet.
Kept her head tucked into folded arms.
Look up, I told her. *Look at the sunflower.*
Look at the cardinal in the picture.

This time she wrote.
The tree it landed on has no leaves.
The yellow in the sunset stings my eyes,
but I can't stop looking at the sparkles.
Something is hiding underneath.

It has a mean mouth and wears a sharp coat.
It is The Color Red.

By the mid 1980s it was clear, after working with enough diverse populations, that poetry can heal people because self-expression can make people feel better. So to reach a broader audience than just students in public and private schools, it became important to work with young people who had been victims of homelessness or abuse.

HARBOR SUMMIT SCHOOL FOR HOMELESS CHILDREN

Students who are homeless are just like any other kids. The difference is that no place is home for them. They've gotten used to always being in transition, since kids are so resilient, but what they cannot get used to is the lack of permanent friendships. They try to make friends, even if it's just for a day, and they hold onto whatever toys are given out at school. They also hold onto pictures they make and poems they write.

The poetry-writing lessons are no different than those used in schools with poor students or rich students or *any* students. None of the lessons presented should encourage them to feel the loss that they live in their everyday lives; however, given the open-endedness of the lessons, some students will, in fact, write about wishing that they could live in a real house, play in their own yard, and make friends that they could keep forever. Some poems will have underlying messages of insecurity, as well. And some, like any typical kid poem, will just reveal an adventurous imagination.

Harbor Summit School was basically a huge room partitioned off with three combined grade-level classes, K–1, 2–3 and 4–5. Students who went there had no consistency in attendance and no academic records. By law, parents had to put their children in school, but since they moved around constantly, the kids had no stable life and, therefore, no stable education. Many were hard to place in a particular grade, and teachers had a difficult time following a curriculum with different kids always showing up.

Students would come to class having not eaten breakfast, which was provided in addition to lunch, possibly their only two meals for the day. They wore whatever clothing their parents could find and frequently hadn't bathed for days or even weeks. Several stayed in shelters. The teacher once pointed out a child who'd been sleeping in a station wagon. Some slept in the riverbed.

Over the year when the poetry-writing workshops took place, students would come and go. Frequently, there were different groups of students from the week before, but the workshops always varied and focused on different elements of poetry. In the end, there was a lot of appreciation. The students enjoyed having poetry brought into their lives, and most relished the opportunity to share their lives. The gift of having a warm place to sleep each night took on a new perspective.

HILLCREST SCHOOL FOR ABUSED AND NEGLECTED WARDS OF THE COURT

When teaching poetry to students who have been abused or neglected by their parents, the lessons for all grade levels need to encourage the students to create worlds that are outside of their awful experiences, to find hope; but of course, they can write whatever they want.

The goal is for them to feel good about writing. Some of their poems will express anger, not just toward their parents, but toward other kids and toward the system that has failed them. They shouldn't censor themselves, though. They should be encouraged to say whatever they want, so that they can feel proud when they express their feelings in poems.

Hillcrest School was a small campus with portable classrooms that looked like low-roofed trailers. The students were assigned to either a second/third-grade class, a fourth/fifth-grade class, or a middle/high-school class. Most of the kids who came there lived in foster care or group homes. They were all removed from their parents' homes because of abuse. Some of them were physically and/or sexually abused and some were simply abandoned or neglected by their parents. Some of the parents were on drugs or were in prison.

Anyone coming into this situation to teach would wonder: what does it feel like to not be loved by one's own parents? At Harbor Summit School, the students had no place to live, and that's scary. But the students who attended Hillcrest School had a home; they just couldn't live there because their parents treated them so badly.

The younger students were quiet, almost withdrawn. They needed to make poetry their friend. Once again, they were like any other kids, so the same lesson plans presented in public schools worked for them. And they wrote like any other kids. They were not encouraged to write about the abuse or neglect, and they usually didn't. They may have been embarrassed by it.

But they did write about make-believe animals and adventures, about friends and siblings, sometimes about grandparents and even about their parents. Most of them loved their parents because they *were* their parents, and they wished for the good life at home. They imagined that. And they took those poems with them.

The middle/high-school class was different. Those were angry students. At first, most of them would not write. They would not even sit in their seats and listen. The goal became getting them to channel all that anger into poems; that would be a miracle. The teacher also had difficulty controlling the class and often bribed them with candy and soda so they would write poems.

One technique that got their attention was to climb on top of the desk and touch the low, trailer ceiling. Then most of them began to listen to the poems read. Eventually, they opened up and wrote. They wrote amazing poems about stuff that interested young teens—boys or girls they had crushes on, wishes to live on their own.

Some of the students at Hillcrest School shared what they wrote, reluctantly, but they would not allow their poems to be copied. Maybe they were afraid they'd get in trouble for telling the truth or for using profanity in their poems. It's understandable why they wouldn't trust anyone to take their poems, why they wouldn't trust any adult to be a caretaker of their words, their lives. The world had betrayed them. The people who were supposed to love them betrayed them. So once again, there were no poems to collect for an anthology.

One day, a girl came to class with bruises all over her body. Her face, particularly, was black and blue, and her hair was chopped short and uneven. The first thought was that one of her parents had done this to her. But she'd been removed from her home. The teacher said that she had been jumped by a gang of girls. So the message this girl got in life was that nowhere was safe, and she had to fight for her life.

It became important to get her to break through and express herself through poetry. But it didn't happen. She hated the world, and that included poetry. No one could blame her for that. But she was there, and although she only wrote one poem, she listened to the poems by professional poets and the poems the students shared. This chapter is dedicated to her, in hopes that life gave her a break and that one day she decided to write.

SAMPLE WRITING EXERCISES

Note: There are no model student poems to use for exercises, so the student poems are from other schools. The lessons used in other schools are the same anyway, since these kids are still kids, just from another side of life. The lesson plans are divided into elementary and secondary grade levels.

Part I: Elementary School

1) Imagination and Personification

Begin by talking about the importance of students using their imagination in poems, and about personification—giving human characteristics to something that's not human. An example would be a chair talking or a tree putting on clothes. The students all give examples, too. After the discussion, read a model poem.

"Maples," by Mary Oliver

The trees have become
suddenly very happy
it is the rain
it is the quick white summer rain

the trees are in motion under it
they are swinging back and forth they are tossing
      the heavy blossoms of their heads
they are twisting their shoulders
even their feet chained to the ground feel good
      thin and gleaming

nobody can prove it but any fool can feel it
they are full of electricity now and the shine isn't just pennies
it pours out from the deepest den
oh pretty trees
      patient   deep-planted

may you have many such days
flinging your bodies in silver circles shaking your heads
over the swamps and the pastures
rimming the fields and the long roads hurrying by.

In this poem, the trees become happy, like people do. Point out that the trees don't really have heads or shoulders, but this poem is rich in pictures and in the use of imagination because of the personification that the poet uses.

Now it's time for students to use their imaginations and write a poem. They can choose an animal or object, something indoors or outdoors, and give it a human life with human features and characteristics. They can also choose a concept if they want.

Here are some student poems from this exercise.

"The Weird Changing," by Karissa, fourth grade

One spring morning in April
a pink bright feathered coat bird,
the beak getting a piece
of a flower. But then it turned night,
the humming bird wasn't a humming bird anymore.
It was turning into a girl
and I was turning into a humming bird.

I was flying with a piece of flower in my mouth.
My voice was gone. My voice was her voice.
From there and that day on
I knew she would have a nice life. And I,
well, I had a rough time flying.

"Sensitivity," by Caitlin, fifth grade

Sensitivity.
It may break like a string.
It may dive out of a soul
and a person may become a wolf
on the prowl for food.
Or possibly it will stay within
the heart and call to people
and beat and beat and beat.
I feel it should stay within forever.
Sensitivity will go on and on
and on like a never-ending string.
Sensitivity.

2) Feelings: The Bully and the Apology

Discuss how it's important to express feelings in poems. Feelings are vital to poems, and it's important to describe them, not just state them. Then read a model poem.

"This Is Just to Say," by William Carlos Williams

I have eaten
the plums
that were in
the icebox

and which
you were probably
saving
for breakfast

Forgive me
they were delicious
so sweet
and so cold

Here, the poet probably wrote this as an apology note to his wife, but it turned out to be a terrific poem. Ask students to think of a time when their feelings were hurt by someone who was being mean to them or bullying them. They can write a poem about that, or they can write a poem apologizing to someone for hurting *his* or *her* feelings.

Here are some student poems expressing feelings.

"Feeling Sad," by Joshua, third grade

I'm feeling sad today because my friends
are calling me names, playing rough, parents
fighting, name on the board and lots of other
things. And because it's raining hard.

"My Apology," by Skyler, third grade

I apologize for
being mean
to you and
after
I was mean I
thought for
a minute and
realized
how mean I was
and I thought
again and realized
that everyone
isn't perfect
and
no one needs to be
treated like
how I treated you.

3) Images: The End of the World

First talk about what images are. Then ask the students to think about what would happen if it were the end of the world. This does not have to be a literal ending. It could be the end of the school year or the end of summer camp or the end of a relationship. The goal is to focus on that theme and to write a poem with images. First read a model poem.

"Halley's Comet," by Stanley Kunitz

Miss Murphy in first grade
wrote its name in chalk
across the board and told us
it was roaring down the stormtracks
of the Milky Way at frightful speed
and if it wandered off its course

and smashed into the earth
there'd be no school tomorrow.
A red-bearded preacher from the hills
with a wild look in his eyes
stood in the public square
at the playground's edge
proclaiming he was sent by God
to save every one of us,
even the little children.
"Repent, ye sinners!" he shouted,
waving his hand-lettered sign.
At supper I felt sad to think
that it was probably
the last meal I'd share
with my mother and my sisters;
but I felt excited too
and scarcely touched my plate.
So mother scolded me
and sent me early to my room.
The whole family's asleep
except for me. They never heard me steal
into the stairwell hall and climb
the ladder to the fresh night air.
Look for me, Father, on the roof
of the red brick building
at the foot of Green Street—
that's where we live, you know, on the top floor.
I'm the boy in the white flannel gown
sprawled on this coarse gravel bed
searching the starry sky,
waiting for the world to end.

Talk about the images that the poet uses, like "it was roaring down the stormtracks" and "I'm the boy in the white flannel gown/ sprawled on this coarse gravel bed/ searching the starry sky." It's easy to see the picture that the poet has created. Then ask the students to write a poem about the end of the world using images.

Here are some student poems with strong images.

"My Dream of the End of the World," by Bethany, fifth grade

My dream of the end
of the world was like the moon
not stealing into the night
it went like this

the room is dark
the bed afloat
and all I see is the dark
of the night slinking
through my room
I hear nothing not even my breathing
I think of nothing
I lie there on my bed
and it starts
to swirl I go down and down
a deep hole I sit up
I'm scared I look around and plunge
into complete darkness
all of a sudden I see light
I see God the end
of the world has come at last
I wake up the sun burns the dark
it was only a dream or was it
I do not know
no one knows the world
could have begun again starting
with me.

"End of the World," by Sasha, fifth grade

If I had the last day to
do anything then I would make sure
I got everything I wanted.
I would make sure nobody was
mean to me.
I would bug my mom until she went crazy
and sit on the couch and watch TV.
Then I'd buy every single dog or cat
but of course I wouldn't buy a mouse
because those cats would probably eat
the mouse, and the dogs would eat
the cats for eating the mice!
Last of all, I would be sure that
no matter how lazy I was I
still had to do my homework.
But then what if there was no school?
Then I would party all day and
forget how to do my math, writing and science!
But I wouldn't forget my reading
or how to do art.

So even if the world did end, I'd
still have to do my homework.
But the world won't end, right?

4) Rhythm: My Worries

Talk about using rhythm in poems by repeating words or lines or by having very short or very long breath lines. Then read a model poem with very short breath lines. Read it in just two or three breaths, and ask the students to snap their fingers to the rhythm.

"Knoxville Tennessee," by Nikki Giovanni

I always like summer
best
you can eat fresh corn
from daddy's garden
and okra
and greens
and cabbage
and lots of
barbecue
and buttermilk
and homemade ice-cream
at the church picnic
and listen to
gospel music
outside
at the church
homecoming
and go to the mountains with
your grandmother
and go barefooted
and be warm
all the time
and only when you go to bed
and sleep

    Everyone enjoys snapping her or his fingers to the poem, and they all understand this kind of rhythm. Talk about how going out to the country like this is a good way to relax and forget their worries. Lots of time people don't know what to do with their worries. Tell the students that they can use their imaginations and get rid of them.
    There are Guatemalan worry dolls that come in a little box. If you can get them, first ask each student to think about his or her worries. Then go around the room and have each student close her or his eyes and imagine a worry

to give to a doll, who will get rid of it like magic. Explain that each doll can only handle up to eight worries, so you are rotating them. This, of course, only works for younger students. If you can't get worry dolls, anything can work, like a dream catcher or even pebbles.

Also talk about other ways students can get rid of their worries. For example, they can tell them to a friend or a pet, or they can drown them in an ocean or lake. Ask the students to write poems that talk about their worries and how they will get rid of them. Ask them to use rhythm in their poems by either repeating lines or words or using very short breath lines.

Here are some student poems with strong rhythm.

"My Golden Heart," by Vanessa, second grade

My worries are locked
in a golden heart
inside me.
My worries flow
through my body.
When I worry
a cold line creeps up
my spine, growing
colder and colder.
It makes me shiver
in the dark.

"Untitled," by Lancin, third grade

I will play my worries into a flute.
And the worries will go
up to the sky. And the sky will give
them to the sun and then the sun
will shine them on the beach
and sink them into the sand.

Sample Exercises—Part II: Middle/High School

1) Imagination and Empathy: Looking Inside Someone to Find Ourselves

Talk about how using the imagination can help poets empathize or feel compassion for another person. When a poet creates a speaker who feels what another person feels and understands her or him in that way, that speaker can relate those things to his or her *own* feelings or experience.

Read model poems where the speakers are intimately involved with someone—a daughter, in the case of Sharon Olds's poem, and other poets in the case of Allen Ginsberg's poem. Both poems clearly show how the speakers can fully relate to another or others. In "The Talk," the speaker finds her daughter drowning inside her. In "A Supermarket in California," the speaker reflects on other poets, particularly Walt Whitman, and calls on him to help shop for images.

"The Talk," by Sharon Olds

In the dark square wooden room at noon
the mother had a talk with her daughter.
The rudeness could not go on, the meanness
to her little brother, the selfishness.
The eight-year-old sat on the bed
in the corner of the room, her irises dark as
the last drops of something, her firm
face melting, reddening,
silver flashes in her eyes like distant
bodies of water glimpsed through woods.
She took it and took it and broke, crying out
I hate being a person! diving
into the mother
as if
into
a deep pond—and she cannot swim,
the child cannot swim.

from "A Supermarket in California," by Allen Ginsberg

What thoughts I have of you tonight, Walt Whitman, for I walked down the sidestreets under the trees with a headache self-conscious looking at the full moon.

In my hungry fatigue, and shopping for images, I went into the neon fruit supermarket, dreaming of your enumerations!

What peaches and what penumbras! Whole families shopping at night! Aisles full of husbands! Wives in the avocados, babies in the tomatoes! —and you, García Lorca, what were you doing down by the watermelons?

I saw you, Walt Whitman, childless, lonely old grubber, poking among the meats in the refrigerator and eyeing the grocery boys.

I heard you asking questions of each: Who killed the pork chops? What price bananas? Are you my Angel?

I wandered in and out of the brilliant stacks of cans following you, and followed in my imagination by the store detective.

We strode down the open corridors together in our solitary fancy tasting artichokes, possessing every frozen delicacy, and never passing the cashier.

Where are we going, Walt Whitman? The doors close in an hour. Which way does your beard point tonight?

Talk about how in the first poem, the mother feels for her daughter. She needs to scold her for her behavior, but the lines,

>
> ... diving
> into the mother
> as if
> into
> a deep pond—and she cannot swim,
> the child cannot swim

clearly show how the daughter lives within the mother, and the mother can feel her pain.

Similarly, in the second poem, the speaker imagines himself taking a journey in a supermarket with other famous poets, Garcia Lorca and Walt Whitman, both of whom are no longer alive. The poem is rich in the use of five senses and details, as the speaker follows Whitman "down the open corridors . . . tasting artichokes . . ."

Now it's time for students to write a poem about someone they either know or have heard about, maybe a great grandmother or someone in history that they've read about. They can either write from that person's perspective or show compassion for what that person has experienced. Tell the students to imagine what that person's life is or was like and how he or she feels or felt about things, to really stretch their imaginations. They can also allow someone to become integrated into their own life, so that they feel like they know this person intimately.

Here's a student poem where the speaker becomes possessed by a person named Bob. The speaker is stepping back and looking at a particular side of herself. Bob is taking over the speaker's mind and is becoming a part of her. She begins to know Bob intimately, but what's haunting about the poem is how Bob is occupying her life.

"Bob," by Dena, sixth grade

I search within my soul to find it,
the happiness I need.
But it is not there, not right now.
Bob. It must be him.
He is the one who drives it away.
I have never felt so much hate for one person.
I chase him away
but he won't leave my head.
He's a bum who has chosen my mind to live in.
I can feel him opening his sleeping bag
and rolling it out onto my mind.
He is a ghost that is haunting me.

He lives with me. I can't get rid of him.
He won't leave me alone.
Almost like a demon
controlling my every thought and wish.
I will try to remove him. I will.
When night's dark beauty reveals itself
I will fight the battle again.

2) Detail: Graffiti Poems

First, talk about why it's important to use details in poetry. Then talk about graffiti. Often people see graffiti as destructive, sometimes gang-related or making a statement against a group of people. But what if graffiti was positive and was made into art? What if people used ideas or little messages that could be posted on walls and made them into poems with great details? They could almost be like found poems—poems that were written as prose, but are really very lyrical and could become poems if they were rewritten with line breaks. Then read a model poem that has no title.

by Jalal ad-Din Muhammed Balkhi ("Rumi"), translated by Coleman Barks

The inspiration you seek
is already within you.
Be silent and listen.

Here, the poet takes three lines to say something very profound that could easily appear on a wall. It forces the reader to stop and think, to "be silent and listen."

Next, read a poem by Frank O'Hara. Again, it could very well appear on a wall somewhere.

"Song," by Frank O'Hara

Is it dirty
does it look dirty
that's what you think of in the city

does it just seem dirty
that's what you think of in the city
you don't refuse to breathe do you

someone comes along with a very bad character
he seems attractive. is he really. yes. very is
he's attractive as his character is bad. is it. yes

that's what you think of in the city
run your finger along your no-moss mind
that's not a thought that's soot

and you take a lot of dirt off someone
is the character less bad. no. it improves constantly
you don't refuse to breathe do you

Talk about the meaning behind this poem as someone commenting on the pollution in the city, most likely a big city. Hold up the poem so the students can notice that there's little punctuation. Talk about how in poetry, they can break the rules of grammar, but they have to know them to break them and have the poem work.

Some poets capitalize the first letter of every word that begins a new line, but more often than not, especially in free verse, poets just capitalize words that begin new sentences or are proper nouns, or in the case of this poem, there is no capitalization beyond the first word. This poem also uses a lot of repetition, creating a strong rhythm throughout the poem.

It's time to write. Tell the students to make up their own graffiti poem, a poem that could be found in a hallway, a subway, or any place else out in the world. But their poems should not be destructive or offensive. Their poems should either celebrate something or make a positive statement. They could use an epigraph, a quote or statement after the title, to tell where the poem can be found. Remind them to use strong, specific details.

Here's a graffiti poem by a student using repetition and clipped language to make his statement—celebrating surfing.

"Surfers Only," by L.R., eighth grade
—written on the seawall at Wind 'n' Sea

No kooks
Locals only
No tourists
If you don't belong
Go home!

You must know the haps
Become committed
A way of life
A custom passed on by
    "Surfers Only"

Appendix
Additional Exercise Ideas

- Begin with "If my Teddy bear could talk . . ."
- Create a new name for yourself. Give it a meaning and a purpose. Start with "My name . . ."
- Slow motion: Describe an action or pretend you're an animal, like a lion or cat, checking out something.
- Think of a magical place. What happens there?
- Who am I deep inside, and who can I imagine myself to be if I were the greatest person in the world? Where would I go and what would I do?
- Write a poem where you dream of peace.
- Start a poem with: "The earth is a living thing."
- Create a secret mission.
- Imagine you are a part of your body, like an ear or your nose, or pretend you are a piece of fruit. View the world from that place.
- Begin with "If my pet/food/whatever could talk . . ."
- Begin with "When I'm sleepy I . . ."
- Begin with "When I'm quiet, I can hear . . ."
- If you were an immigrant or moving somewhere, what would you bring?
- Look at an object in a new way. What does a house represent? An orange? A shoe? And so on.
- Start a poem with "I never saw. . ."
- Imagine you're the grass or the snow, and so on. Describe that experience.
- Think of a time someone made you cry. What happened?
- Become the sense of smell, touch, sound, or taste. Write from that perspective; for example, "My name is touch, and I love hugging."
- Become an emotion. What do you do? For example, "I am hate. I pick on people."

- Look inside a desk drawer. What do you find? For example, you find a letter. What does it say?
- Describe the room through only one of the five senses.
- Describe an everyday occurrence, such as a sunset or rain, in an unusual way using images and metaphors or similes.
- When animals die, what do you do? Do you have a ritual to perform? How do you deal with the loss?

Permissions

Robert Bly, "A Late Spring Day in my Life" from *Silence in the Snowy Fields*, Wesleyan University Press, Middletown, CT, 1962. Copyright © 1962 by Robert Bly. Used with permission of the author.

California Poets in the Schools (CPITS) student poems that have appeared in their anthologies: "Fights," by Joel Samudio, "The Most Amazing Thing I Ever Saw," by Brett Sawyer, "Being A Rock," by Christie Medina, "Sadness," by Maria Cervantes, "Red Rat," by Shannon Jones, "Alone in My House," by Alicia Menchaca, "Right Back Home," by Jonathan Sessa, "Columbine," by Flavio Cruz, "Why Is There War?" by Clay Morris, "Grease Refuses to Slide in the Machinery of Progress," by Bill Powers, "The Wages of Dying Is Love," by Heather Foyer, "My Sister," by Isabelle Moore, "The Weird Changing," by Karissa Morales, "My Dream of the End of the World," by Bethany Angelette, "The Shooting Field," by Jajie Darden, "Drowning in Him," by Becky Rodkin, "Apathy," by Laura Suval, "Cowboy Bill," by Evelyn Belasco, and "Father," by Cameron Brooks. California Poets in the Schools grants permission to use these student poems. This book was made possible in part by the student poems that are a result of the CPITS program, and the book is produced in part to promote the CPITS mission.

Robert Frost, "Stopping by Woods on a Snowy Evening" from the book THE POETRY OF ROBERT FROST, edited by Edward Connery Lathem. Copyright © 1923, 1969 by Henry Holt and Company, copyright © 1951 by Robert Frost. Reprinted by permission of Henry Holt and Company, LLC. All rights reserved.

Allen Ginsberg, excerpt of 8 lines from "A Supermarket in California" from COLLECTED POEMS 1947–1980. Copyright © 1955 by Allen Ginsberg. Reprinted by permission of HarperCollins Publishers.

Nikki Giovanni, "Knoxville, Tennessee" from BLACK FEELING, BLACK TALK, BLACK JUDGMENT. Copyright © 1968, 1970 by NIKKI GIOVANNI. Reprinted by permission of HarperCollins Publishers.

Donald Hall, "Self-Portrait As A Bear" from OLD AND NEW POEMS. Copyright © 1990 by Donald Hall. Reprinted by permission of Houghton Mifflin Harcourt Publishing Company. All rights reserved.

Sam Hamill, "Three Worlds" from *Gratitude*. Copyright © 1998 by Sam Hamill. Used by permission of the author.

Ruth Hanley has granted permission to use excerpts from her letter dated June 17, 2012.

Langston Hughes, "Poem [2]" from THE COLLECTED POEMS OF LANGSTON HUGHES, edited by Arnold Rampersad with David Roessel, Associate Editor, copyright © 1994 by the Estate of Langston Hughes. Used by permission of Alfred A. Knopf, an imprint of the Knopf Doubleday Publishing Group, a division of Penguin Random House LLC. All rights reserved.

Galway Kinnell, "Little Sleep's-Head Sprouting in the Moonlight" from THE BOOK OF NIGHTMARES. Copyright © 1971, renewed 1999 by Galway Kinnell. Reprinted by permission of Houghton Mifflin Harcourt Publishing Company. All rights reserved.

Yusef Komunyakaa, "Facing It" from *Dien Cai Dau*. Copyright © 1988 by Yusef Komunyakaa. Reprinted with permission of Wesleyan University Press.

Maxine Kumin, "The Hermit Picks Berries." Copyright © 1972 by Maxine Kumin, from SELECTED POEMS 1960–1990. Used by permission of the author and W. W. Norton & Company, Inc.

Stanley Kunitz, "Halley's Comet." Copyright © 1995 by Stanley Kunitz, and "The Portrait." Copyright © 1971 by Stanley Kunitz, from THE COLLECTED POEMS. Used by permission of the author and W. W. Norton & Company, Inc.

Denise Levertov, "Moon Tiger" from POEMS 1968–1972, copyright © 1968 by Denise Levertov. Reprinted by permission of New Directions Publishing Corp.

Peter Levitt, "The Boat" from *Bright Root, Dark Root*, Broken Moon Press. Copyright © 1991 by Peter Levitt. Used by permission of the author.

Federico Garcia Lorca, "The Moon Rising" translated by Lysander Kemp, from THE SELECTED POEMS OF FEDERICO GARCIA LORCA, copyright © 1955 by New Directions Publishing Corp. Reprinted by permission of New Directions Publishing Corp.

Glenna Luschei, "Dream of Snow" from *Salt Lick*. Copyright © 2009 by Glenna Luschei. Used with permission of the author.

W. S. Merwin, "Crossing Place" from FLOWER AND HAND. Copyright © 1997 by W. S. Merwin, used by permission of The Wylie Agency LLC.

Naomi Shihab Nye, "Mad" from *Come with Me: Poems for a Journey*, © 2000 by Naomi Shihab Nye. Used by permission of the author, Naomi Shihab Nye, 2015.

Frank O'Hara, "Autobiographia Literaria," and "Song (is It Dirty)" from THE COLLECTED POEMS OF FRANK O'HARA, copyright © 1971 by Maureen Granville-Smith, Administratrix of the Estate of Frank O'Hara, copyright renewed 1999 by Maureen O'Hara Granville-Smith and Donald Allen. Used by permission of Alfred A. Knopf, an imprint of the Knopf Doubleday Publishing Group, a division of Penguin Random House LLC. All rights reserved.

Dwight Okita, "IN RESPONSE TO EXECUTIVE ORDER 9066: All Americans of Japanese Descent Must Report to Relocation Centers" from *Crossing with the*

Light (Tia Chucha Press, 1992.) Copyright © 1992 by Dwight Okita. Reprinted by permission of the author.

Sharon Olds, "The Talk" from *Satan Says*, copyright © 1980 by Sharon Olds. Reprinted by permission of the University of Pittsburgh Press.

Mary Oliver, "Maples" from WEST WIND: Poems and Prose Poems. Copyright © 1997 by Mary Oliver. Reprinted by permission of Houghton Mifflin Harcourt Publishing Company. All rights reserved.

Alicia Susan Ostriker, "It rains it thaws" from the poem sequence "Almanac" from *The Book of Seventy*, copyright © 2009 by Alicia Susan Ostriker. Reprinted by permission of the University of Pittsburgh Press.

Linda Pastan, "Pass/Fail," from ASPECTS OF EVE. Copyright © 1970, 1971, 1972, 1973, 1974, 1975 by Linda Pastan. Used by permission of Liveright Publishing Corporation.

Kenneth Patchen, "The Magical Mouse" from COLLECTED POEMS OF KENNETH PATCHEN, copyright © 1957 by New Directions Publishing Corp. Reprinted by permission of New Directions Publishing Corp.

Marge Piercy, "Outcome of the matter: The sun" from CIRCLES ON THE WATER, copyright © 1982 by Middlemarsh, Inc. Used by permission of Alfred A. Knopf, an imprint of the Knopf Doubleday Publishing Group, a division of Penguin Random House LLC. All rights reserved.

Jalal ad-Din Rumi, ". . . the inspiration you seek" translated by Coleman Barks. Copyright © by Coleman Barks. Used by permission of Coleman Barks.

Shelley Savren, "Welcome to Poetryland," "Trees Green around the Shed," and "The Court School" from *The Wild Shine of Oranges* (Tebot Bach Press). Copyright © 2013 by Shelley Savren. Used by permission of the author.

Shelley Savren, "The Star" and "Shepherd Girl." Copyright © 2015 by Shelley Savren. Used by permission of the author.

Charles Simic, "Stone" from *Dismantling The Silence*. Copyright © 1971 by Charles Simic. Used by permission of the author.

Gary Snyder, "Running Water Music II" from REGARDING WAVE, copyright © 1970 by Gary Snyder. Reprinted by permission of New Directions Publishing Corp.

Gary Soto, "Ode to Pablo's Tennis Shoes" from NEIGHBORHOOD ODES: Poems by Gary Soto. Text copyright © 1992 by Gary Soto. Reprinted by permission of Houghton Mifflin Harcourt Publishing Company. All rights reserved.

Wallace Stevens, "Six Significant Landscapes" from THE COLLECTED POEMS OF WALLACE STEVENS, copyright © 1954 by Wallace Stevens and copyright renewed 1982 by Holly Stevens. Used by permission of Alfred A. Knopf, an imprint of the Knopf Doubleday Publishing Group, a division of Penguin Random House LLC. All rights reserved.

Amy Uyematsu, "One More October" from *The Yellow Door*. Copyright © 2015 by Amy Uyematsu. Used by permission of Red Hen Press.

William Carlos Williams, "The Red Wheelbarrow" and "This is Just to Say" from THE COLLECTED POEMS: VOLUME I, 1909–1939, copyright © 1938 by New Directions Publishing Corp. Reprinted by permission of New Directions Publishing Corp.

Resources

American Academy of Poets: www.poets.org
Association of Writers and Writing Programs: www.awpwriter.org
California Poets in the Schools: www.cpits.org
Poetry Foundation: www.poetryfoundation.org
Poetry Out Loud: www.poetryoutloud.org
Poets and Writers: www.pw.org
Teachers and Writers Collaborative: www.twc.org

Index

alliteration, 12, 37, 38
"Almanac: It rains it thaws" (Alicia Ostriker), 60
"Autobiographia Literaria" (Frank O'Hara), 7

"A Birthday" (Christina Rossetti), 62
"The Boat" (Peter Levitt), 40–41
Bly, Robert:
   "A Late Spring Day in My Life," 31

color, 3, 9–10, 20, 27, 28, 41, 80, 81, 91–93
"The Court School" (Shelley Savren), 97
craft, 14
"Crossing Place" (W. S. Merwin), 36

details, 9, 25, 37, 38, 74, 82, 109, 110
"Dream of Snow" (Glenna Luschei), 90

"Facing It" (Yusef Komunyakaa), 48
feelings (emotions), 10, 28, 42, 61, 70, 93, 102
five senses (perception), 9, 23, 24, 35, 36, 78
form, 12, 50
Frost, Robert:
   "Stopping by Woods on a Snowy Evening," 38

Ginsberg, Allen:
   from "A Supermarket in California," 107, 108
Giovanni, Nikki:
   "Knoxville Tennessee," 106

Hall, Donald:
   "Self-Portrait As A Bear," 22
"Halley's Comet" (Stanley Kunitz), 103–104
Hamill, Sam:
   "Three Worlds," 92
"The Hermit Picks Berries" (Maxine Kumin), 27
Hughes, Langston:
   "Poem," 61

"I Hear America Singing" (Walt Whitman), 34
imagery, 10–11, 44–47, 69–70, 81–82, 89–91
imagination, 5, 8, 9, 10, 21, 33, 44, 60, 69, 87, 100, 107
"IN RESPONSE TO EXECTIVE ORDER 9066 All Americans of Japanese Descent Must Report to Relocation Centers" (Dwight Okita), 43

"the inspiration you seek. . ." (Jalal ad-Din Rumi, trans. Coleman Barks), 110

Kinnell, Galway:
 from Little Sleep's-Head Sprouting Hair In The Moonlight," 50, 52, 53
"Knoxville Tennessee" (Nikki Giovanni), 106
Komunyakaa, Yusef:
 "Facing It," 48
Kumin, Maxine, 12;
 "The Hermit Picks Berries," 27
Kunitz, Stanley:
 "Halley's Comet," 103–104

"A Late Spring Day in My Life" (Robert Bly), 31
Levertov, Denise, 67;
 "Moon Tiger," 29
Levitt, Peter:
 "The Boat," 40–41
 "Little Sleep's-Head Sprouting Hair In The Moonlight" (Galway Kinnell), 50–51
Lorca, Federico Garcia, trans. Lysander Kemp:
 "The Moon Rising," 94
Luschei, Glenna:
 "Dream of Snow," 90

Merwin, W. S.:
 "Crossing Place," 36
 "Mad" (Naomi Shihab Nye), 59
 "The Magical Mouse" (Kenneth Patchen), 32–33
"Maples" (Mary Oliver), 101
metaphor, 11, 39, 41
"The Moon Rising" (Federico Garcia Lorca, trans. Lysander Kemp), 94
"Moon Tiger" (Denise Levertov), 29

Nye, Naomi Shihab:
 "Mad," 59

"Ode to Pablo's Tennis Shoes" (Gary Soto), 83–84
O'Hara, Frank:
 "Autobiographia Literaria," 7;
 "Song," 110
Okita, Dwight:
 "IN RESPONSE TO EXECTIVE ORDER 9066 All Americans of Japanese Descent Must Report to Relocation Centers," 43
Olds, Sharon, 107;
 "The Talk," 108
Oliver, Mary, 12;
 "Maples," 101
"One More October" (Amy Uyematsu), 24
Ostriker, Alicia:
 "Almanac: It rains it thaws," 60

"Pass/Fail" (Linda Pastan), 45–46
Pastan, Linda:
 "Pass/Fail," 45–46
Patchen, Kenneth (The Magical Mouse"), 32–33
persona, 11–12, 42– 44, 81–82
personification, 11, 12, 39, 41, 72, 100
Piercy, Marge:
 from "The Total Influence or Outcome of the Matter: THE SUN," 81
"Poem" (Langston Hughes), 61

"The Red Wheelbarrow" (William Carlos Williams), 80
revision, 14, 20
rhythm, 12, 32, 33, 47, 48, 49, 58, 59, 67, 86, 106, 107
Rossetti, Christina:
 from "A Birthday," 62
Rumi, Jalal ad-Din, trans. Coleman Barks:
 "The inspiration you seek. . . ," 110
"Running Water Music II" (Gary Snyder), 88

Savren, Shelley:
   "The Court School," 97;
   "The Shepherd Girl," 85–86;
   "The Star," 77;
   "Trees Green around the Shed," 55;
   "Welcome to Poetryland," 17
"Self-Portrait As A Bear" (Donald Hall), 22
"The Shepherd Girl" (Shelley Savren), 85–86
Simic, Charles:
   "Stone," 26
simile, 11, 31, 32, 39, 40, 41, 62, 63
"Six Significant Landscapes" (Wallace Stevens), 30
Snyder, Gary:
   "Running Water Music II," 88
"Song" (Frank O'Hara), 100
"Song of Myself," section 26 (Walt Whitman), 78–79
Soto, Gary:
   "Ode to Pablo's Tennis Shoes," 83–84
"The Star" (Shelley Savren), 77
Stevens, Wallace:
   from "Six Significant Landscapes," 30
"Stone" (Charles Simic), 26

"Stopping by Woods on a Snowy Evening," (Robert Frost), 38
"Supermarket in California" (Allen Ginsberg), 108

"The Talk" (Sharon Olds), 108
"This Is Just To Say" (William Carlos Williams), 102
"Three Worlds" (Sam Hamill), 92
"Total Influence or Outcome of the Matter: THE SUN" (Marge Piercy), 81
"Trees Green around the Shed" (Shelley Savren), 55

Uyematsu, Amy:
   "One More October," 24

"Welcome to Poetryland" (Shelley Savren), 17
Whitman, Walt:
   "I Hear America Singing," 34;
   from "Song of Myself" (section 26), 78–79
Williams, William Carlos:
   "The Red Wheelbarrow," 80;
   "This Is Just To Say," 102

About the Author

Since January 1976, **Shelley Savren** has taught poetry-writing workshops to over twenty-five thousand people, including pre-K through college students, homeless children, abused and neglected youth, adolescents with mental health issues, and developmentally disabled adults. She has taught in hundreds of classrooms, including a maximum-security men's prison, juvenile halls, art museums, a senior center, and women's centers. Ms. Savren's workshops have been featured in several newspapers, such as *The Los Angeles Times*, *The Ventura County Star*, and *The San Diego Union-Tribune*, which has written, "By helping people know the world about them, perceive it with all of their senses, Shelley Savren helps them stretch their imaginations."

Ms. Savren is the author of two poetry collections, *The Common Fire* (Red Hen Press, 2004) and *The Wild Shine of Oranges* (Tebot Bach Press, 2013). Her poetry has been published widely in literary magazines, including *Prairie Schooner*, *Solo*, *Rattle*, *Main Street Rag*, *Solstice: A Magazine of Diverse Voices*, and *Serving House Journal*, and she has read at universities, libraries, and coffee houses across the United States.

Ms. Savren's awards include the John David Johnson Memorial Poetry Award, Rainer Marie Rilke International Poetry Competition, Cleveland State University Poetry Center Prize (finalist for *The Common Fire*), and University of Arkansas Press Poetry Series Prize (semi-finalist for *The Wild Shine of Oranges*). She has received nine California Arts Council Artist in Residence grants, three National Endowment for the Arts regional grants, five artist fellowships from the City of Ventura, and a nomination for a Pushcart Prize.

About the Author

Ms. Savren has conducted many in-service workshops for teachers and trained dozens of poets to conduct poetry-writing workshops. She is a fellow of the South Coast Writing Project, an affiliated site of the California and National Writing Project, and holds a BA from Ohio State University, an MA from Central Michigan University, and an MFA from Antioch University, Los Angeles. She is a professor emeritus of English and creative writing at Oxnard College, Oxnard, California. Visit her website at www.shelleysavren.com.

www.ingramcontent.com/pod-product-compliance
Lightning Source LLC
Chambersburg PA
CBHW020748230426
43665CB00009B/536